Foundations of Medieval History
General Editor M.T. Clanchy

Foundations of Medieval History

The Medieval Reformation

Brenda Bolton

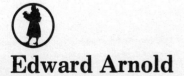

Edward Arnold

© Brenda Bolton 1983

First published in Great Britain 1983
by Edward Arnold (Publishers) Ltd
41 Bedford Square
London WC1 3DQ

Edward Arnold (Australia) Pty Ltd
80 Waverly Road
Caulfield East 3145
PO Box 234
Melbourne

First Published in United States of America 1983
by Edward Arnold
300 North Charles Street
Baltimore
Maryland 21201

British Library Cataloguing in Publication Data

Bolton, Brenda
  The Medieval reformation.—(Foundations of Medieval History).
  1. Church history—Middle Ages, 600—1500.
  I. Title   II. Series
  270.4   BR227

  ISBN 0-7131-6252-X

Text set in 10/12 pt Century Schoolbook
by Colset Private Limited, Singapore
Printed and Bound in Great Britain by
Richard Clay (The Chaucer Press) Ltd,
Bungay, Suffolk

Contents

General preface

The purpose of this series is to provide concise and authoritative introductions to fundamental developments in medieval history. The books are designed to enable students both to master the basic facts about a topic and to form their own point of view. The authors, on their side, have an opportunity to write at greater length — and with more freedom — than in a chapter of a general textbook and, at the same time, to reach out to a wider audience than a specialist monograph commands.

In the present book Brenda Bolton discusses the idea of a medieval Reformation. She shows that there was a deep religious crisis in western Christendom in the twelfth century, just as there was in the sixteenth, although divided Churches were not its outcome. There was a desire to return to the simplicity of the apostolic life of the New Testament and a dissatisfaction with traditional religious practice. Out of this ferment emerged not warring sects, as in the sixteenth-century Reformation, but a variety of religious orders all owing obedience to the pope: Augustinians, Cistercians, Dominicans, Franciscans and many others. Only the Cathars and some of the Waldensians were excluded. This policy of authoritarian inclusiveness was largely the achievement of Pope Innocent III, who had the confidence to welcome the originality of St Francis while at the same time promoting crusades to destroy heretics and pagans. In such a policy there were of course contradictions and tensions, but the author suggests that harnessing the energies of lay men — and women — to the purposes of the universal Church was a new and considerable achievement which re-formed the civilization of medieval Europe.

M.T. Clanchy

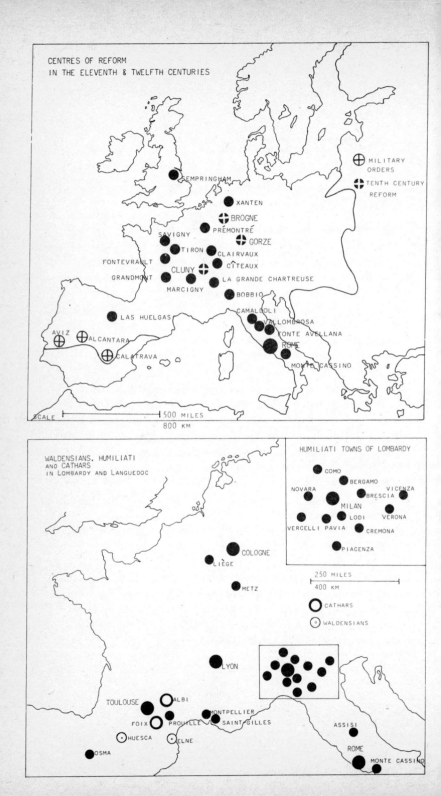

CENTRES OF REFORM
IN THE ELEVENTH & TWELFTH CENTURIES

⊕ MILITARY
ORDERS

⊕ TENTH CENTURY
REFORM

SEMPRINGHAM

XANTEN

BROGNE

PRÉMONTRÉ

SAVIGNY

GORZE

TIRON

CLAIRVAUX

FONTEVRAULT

CÎTEAUX

CLUNY

GRANDMONT

LA GRANDE CHARTREUSE

MARCIGNY

BOBBIO

LAS HUELGAS

CAMALDOLI

VALLOMBROSA

AVIZ   ALCANTARA

FONTE AVELLANA

ROME

CALATRAVA

MONTE CASSINO

SCALE ⊢————— 500 MILES

800 KM

WALDENSIANS, HUMILIATI
AND CATHARS
IN LOMBARDY AND LANGUEDOC

HUMILIATI TOWNS OF LOMBARDY

COMO

BERGAMO

NOVARA

VICENZA

BRESCIA

MILAN

VERCELLI PAVIA LODI VERONA

CREMONA

PIACENZA

250 MILES

400 KM

◯ CATHARS

⊙ WALDENSIANS

COLOGNE

LIÈGE

METZ

LYON

TOULOUSE

ALBI

FOIX

MONTPELLIER

PROUILLE SAINT-GILLES

HUESCA   ELNE

ASSISI

OSMA

ROME

MONTE CASSINO

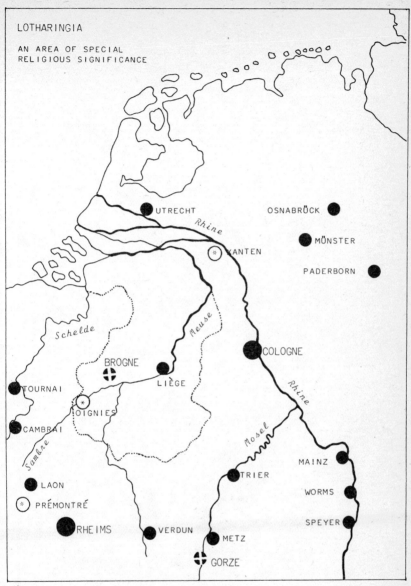

LOTHARINGIA

AN AREA OF SPECIAL
RELIGIOUS SIGNIFICANCE

UTRECHT

OSNABRÜCK

MÜNSTER

XANTEN

PADERBORN

Rhine

Schelde

Meuse

BROGNE

LIÈGE

COLOGNE

Rhine

TOURNAI

OIGNIES

Sambre

CAMBRAI

Mosel

TRIER

MAINZ

LAON

WORMS

PRÉMONTRÉ

SPEYER

RHEIMS

VERDUN

METZ

GORZE

✠ TENTH CENTURY REFORMING CENTRES

✳ TWELFTH CENTURY PREACHERS AND CANONS

SCALE ├─────────────────────┤

250 MILES
400 KM

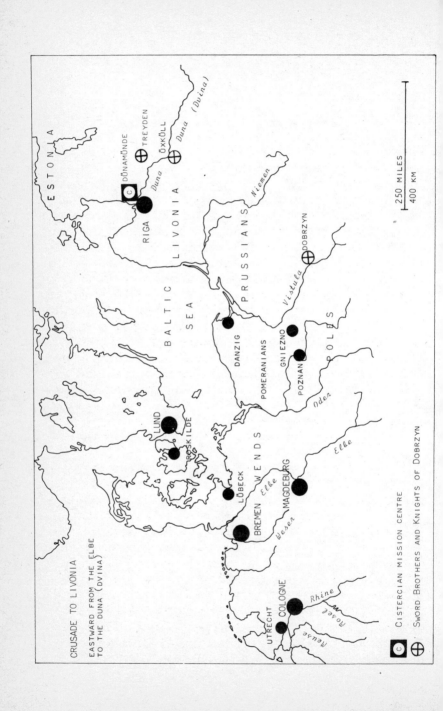

CRUSADE TO LIVONIA

EASTWARD FROM THE ELBE
TO THE DUNA (DVINA)

🅲 CISTERCIAN MISSION CENTRE

⊕ SWORD BROTHERS AND KNIGHTS OF DOBRZYN

250 MILES
400 KM

ESTONIA

LIVONIA

Duna (Dvina)

TREYDEN
ÜXKÜLL
DÜNAMÜNDE
Duna
RIGA

BALTIC   SEA

PRUSSIANS

Niemen

DOBRZYN
Vistula

POLES

DANZIG

POMERANIANS

GNIEZNO

POZNAN

Oder

LUND

ROSKILDE

WENDS

Elbe

LÜBECK

Elbe

MAGDEBURG

BREMEN

Weser

Elbe

UTRECHT

COLOGNE

Rhine

Meuse

Mosel

Introduction

Among today's standard textbooks in medieval history are many which portray certain characteristics of the twelfth century in terms which have usually been associated with the fifteenth and sixteenth centuries alone. These characteristics, reflecting both humanism and naturalism, were concerned with the revival in the twelfth century of ideas which had previously belonged to classical and patristic times. These were accompanied by an increasing awareness of history and its perspective and indicated such an atmosphere of renewal and rebirth as to justify the designation 'Twelfth Century Renaissance'. Some historians try to go even further. Contemporary literature and poetry lead them to identify the twelfth century as one in which the individual was increasingly important. Still more stress the flowering of communities and groups in which aims and values, held in common by their members, created varying forms of corporate awareness, differentiated one from another by the terms in which the members of each community or group saw themselves. The common inspiration underlying this variety of different individuals, communities and groups was to be found in the spiritual and religious revival occurring at the time.

So great was this spiritual ferment and so altered was men's conception of the Christian life and its purpose in the world, that some historians of medieval spirituality consider it to be a change as fundamental, as deep and as lasting as the Reformation of the sixteenth century. With such a similarity, yet another designation of twelfth century characteristics may now be appropriate; that is of a 'twelfth century reformation' which in itself formed part of a wider Medieval Reformation covering the years between *c.* 1050 and 1226, the latter year coinciding with the death of St Francis. As in the sixteenth century, there existed in the twelfth an acute awareness of the danger which had faced the Church since Gospel times through repeated attempts to form, deform, reform, deform and reform yet again in line with the fashion of the period. These two reformation periods, however, reflected deeper spiritual and religious revivals which were marked by the activities both of evangelical preachers and of laymen whose determined demand to be allowed to read and preach the Scriptures for themselves affected all sections of society. This led to a concentration on the consequences of sin, on the way to obtain personal salvation and on the manner in which Christian life ought to be lived. Renunciation of the world, followed by isolation in a life of prayer, was no longer to be the only path to salvation, although, particularly in the twelfth century, such a renunciation was still considered by many to be meritorious and important. The striking development of religious orders allowing such a way of life indicated its great power to attract and recompense those large numbers of recruits who entered monasteries and religious houses in order to attain it. The other increasingly more appealing path was through a renewed emphasis on the obligation to live a Christian life in the world, serving God, loving and serving one's neighbours through charity, not only by caring for the poor and sick and in spreading education but also by engaging in mission as ambassadors for Christ in the care of souls and their salvation. These obligations were undertaken with so much enthusiasm and determination that in both centuries men were willing to participate, even to the extent of being eager to fight to defend and propagate the faith when called upon to do so. The twelfth century call may have been a crusade, authorized by the pope on behalf of the one universal Church; whilst that of the sixteenth century, a call for men to support the missions of sects and separated churches, was often against the doctrinal control of the papacy. The intensity of their faith was equally strong.

These spiritual reawakenings profoundly affected all aspects of religious life but there was to be no such startling or dramatic conclusion to the events of the twelfth century as that which occurred in the sixteenth. The 'Reformation' has thus traditionally been interpreted as that religious movement, led chiefly by Martin Luther, concerned with the revival of the biblical doctrine of access by faith into grace and which took place over a wide area of western Christendom in the sixteenth century. The term is so popularly linked with those religious beliefs, attitudes and institutions which came from the reformed and protestant Churches of that time that it conjures up a picture of a Church completely separated from Rome. Such was the concentration on the implications of atonement, the doctrine of grace and justification by faith and on the importance of the priesthood of all believers that questions of morals and administration in the Christian life and the Christian Church were obscured by this stark commitment to doctrine. Twelfth century events had not fully pioneered that particular road. There, the search for reform whilst not neglecting doctrinal matters, specially amongst some groups, had perhaps been more concerned with the development of a personal way of life, with corresponding consequences for the administration and future organization of the Church, that institution to which all Christians belonged. The characteristics of the twelfth century in terms of 'reformation' or *reformatio* can best be explained in the two descriptions of reform put forward by Giles Constable: the first, backward-looking and returning to an original ideal — the time of Christ and the apostles: the second, forward-looking to a reformed existence — the kingdom of God. Both these views are typical of the religious ferment of the twelfth century. The Church emerged changed, renewed and reformed but although it was not faced with a challenge from any alternative institution to its position at the centre of western Christendom, a reformation had nevertheless taken place.

Those parts of Christendom which were most relevant at this time of spiritual change were the lands of France, Italy and Norman England, in all of which the rulers were mainly Romance-speaking. The bilingual borderlands of the Low Countries and Empire, between the rivers Rhine, Meuse and Moselle, still called Lotharingia by contemporaries, formed an area of special religious significance. During the twelfth century the frontiers of this whole region became more secure than they had ever been. The Magyar threat to the east had long since been averted and the Scandinavian kingdoms to the north had been firmly christianized. Poland, Bohemia and Hungary were eager to establish relations not only with the papacy but also with France and England. In the south two-thirds of Spain had been reconquered from the Moslems whilst the Christian kingdoms of Castile and Aragon had been firmly established. In all, the region was fairly compact geographically with a long-standing ecclesiastical tradition based on Rome. The only exception occurred on the eastern frontier where the Germans had resumed their push from the Rhine to the Elbe and beyond, and where their penetration along the southern Baltic shores became associated not only with the northern crusades but

also with monastic missions to Livonia and to Prussia. At the
frontiers of the whole region were many sensitive points where
both christianization and colonization were possible and which
could reflect the spiritual developments which were taking place
within.

These spiritual developments, although occurring mainly in the
twelfth century, started in the latter part of the eleventh and were
carried on throughout the twelfth and into the first part of the
thirteenth. They reflected the economic, social and political
changes of the time and strikingly, the demand for these changes,
although concerned with religious beliefs and experience and
expressed as they were through religious institutions, often
originated from the laity, a laity in which women played an important role. It was only to be expected that there would be a desire for
those changes taking place in material life to be paralleled by
changes in the concept of the religious life and there was
considerable dissatisfaction with the lack of spiritual lead being
given by the institutionalized Church in this direction. The desire
for these changes did not diminish the expansion of existing institutions. In a period of great economic growth, it was only to be
expected that developments could take place in a variety of directions, some for change, some for strengthening existing traditions. At the beginning of this period the papacy, the secular
Church with its diocesan structure of archbishops, bishops and
priests and the regular Church with its monks in their autonomous
and vaguely related monasteries, were the institutions through
which traditional religious experience, awareness and activities
were expressed. Together they formed the one Church of Christ to
which all belonged. As new spiritual questions arose, they were to
face a period of stress and strain, of ferment and awakening and an
awareness of history different in the twelfth century from any
which had come before. It appeared to many that in a large number
of ways these institutions had ceased to cater for developing
aspirations and expectations. A particular feature of the time was
that men and women were tempted to seek new means by which
such institutions could be bypassed.

Although the aim of the Church was to maintain its purpose and
function it needed to be able to adjust its beliefs and institutions to
meet the demands being made upon it. Unchanged it would not be
able to match spiritual aspirations, and extraneous alternatives
might appear and prosper. At the beginning of the period it was

hoped that reforms initiated by the papacy and the codification of canon law might deal with the problem but this was not to be so. A long and continually changing crisis occurred, often highlighted by the beliefs and actions of many differing individuals and groups but perhaps the most significant institutional response to a religious life, at once systematic and yet more spiritual and apostolic, came with the founding and growth of organized monastic orders, inspirationally new and widespread and theologically based but always inside the existing Church. The success of these new orders and the greater sympathy and understanding shown to lay groups eventually allowed the Church, when Innocent III was pope, to present a further reformed stance which the decisions of the Fourth Lateran Council of 1215 attempted to formalize. Inevitably, once these decisions had been made, pressure reappeared from many directions for still more far-reaching reform. Yet the tolerance evident in the twelfth century did not carry over for very long into the thirteenth. What was then considered to be heresy was totally suppressed and any move towards a separation of Churches was, for the time being, quelled. The twelfth-century variety of attempts to find a successful method of reform was thus rather a significant sign of important times than a thoroughgoing Reformation. That had to wait for other more determined forces in different circumstances to bring it about in future years.

This book has been given chronological limits but it is not strictly chronological in approach. The contents are best regarded as a series of broadly drawn pictures of relevant subjects, areas and samples focusing on important events, movements and groups with interrelated reactions and indicating what was going on during the whole period. In this way a fuller understanding may be achieved of the historical and theological bases for the spiritual reawakening which occurred.

The material from which this book has been compiled is to be found in a great number of other books and articles but the connected theme employed here and the overall comparative approach are perhaps not to be found elsewhere. It is an attempt at a general introduction to the subject for interested students: a synthesis of currently existing research. Numerous specialist books may be used as a basis for extended reading in any particular direction and many of these can be found in the further reading list at the end of the book.

1
The religious crisis of the twelfth century

Beginning in the late eleventh century and developing in the course of the twelfth, there occurred a recognizable shift of religious emphasis — the infusion of a new zeal and vigour. Whereas withdrawal from the world had hitherto been the recognized way by which Christians might achieve a holy and spiritual life for God, there was now stress on the importance of an evangelical entry into the world. Henceforth, the life of Christ and his apostles was to be the example, with the Church influencing the world, organizing it and leading it to salvation. This shift was so widespread amongst those in monasteries and even amongst the laity, and marked so significant a turning point in medieval spirituality that it has been justly termed by historians the religious crisis of the twelfth century. Within this general crisis of changing spirituality there were resulting particular crises influencing and affecting the whole of religious life in western Christendom and giving rise in turn to a considerable ferment of ideas. The range of questions asked and the authorities appealed to in seeking to find what the gospels and the early Church Fathers really meant were so enlarged by the crisis that the idea of an all-embracing system of established theological truth, often resulting in codification in canon law, was slowly fashioned.

This awakening study of the Gospel by the whole social body of the Church during the twelfth century penetrated the Christian mystery with controversies regarding intellectual and institutional behaviour so that Christian people became collectively more and more aware of their environment and sought to rationalize it. Individually too, there was a new self-awareness which followed Christ's condemnation of the sin in the heart and led to an awakening of the importance of conscience. Sin was no longer to be just a matter of external actions with penitential counteractions but was also to be a matter of unspoken internal intention and internal contrition where the need for the grace of Christ for salvation was perhaps more important than it had been in recent

17

times. It is perhaps no accident that this crisis in spirituality corresponded to the agrarian and urban preparations for the expansion of Europe which were also taking place in different spheres during the twelfth century.

Roots of the crisis

The period on either side of the appointment of Gregory VII (1073–1085) as pope saw many measures to reform the Church and to elucidate its role in relation to the empire. The essence of these reforms covered what was considered to be wrong with the Church and what was ineffective about the world position of the pope. The Church had become lax and worldly in its activities. Simony, that is the abuse of buying and selling ecclesiastical office, was rife and laymen exerted a disproportionate influence over Church appointments. Similarly, the papacy either followed too closely the way of life of certain rich Roman families or was too much under the control of the emperor. The remedies put forward to deal with this situation were the isolation of the clergy accompanied by the elevation of the sacerdotal office, control of clerical offices and the enforcement of clerical celibacy in monasteries or in similar institutions and, most importantly, the removal of lay interference from clerical appointments. The pope became more independent by clearly defining the rights and responsiblities of the papacy, by the substitution of Roman canon law for Germanic Church Law and by guaranteeing the freedom of election to the office of pope.

This programme of reform was in the hands of the most advanced reforming group of the day. The group included the pope and many of his cardinals all of whom were possibly influenced by the reforming ideas emanating from the monasteries of Cluny, Brogne and Gorze. It presented what could be seen as a form of revolution by a return to an idealized view of an earlier Church, the *ecclesia primitiva* of the apostles. Yet such a programme was difficult to implement. The difference between the actual primitive Church and the elaborate administrative machinery set up to realize the aims of papal advancement was so great as to cause them to be in direct opposition to each other. As the reforms progressed it became increasingly difficult to conceal this disparity. For a while a rupture between the two wings of the reform movement was avoided as the more extreme elements were successfully contained by the extraordinary personal prestige and administrative skills of Gregory VII and also of Urban II (1088–1099). As the papacy moved further from the aim of apostolic asceticism to that of administrative effectiveness this reaction could no longer be contained. The full consequences were to develop later and play their part in the religious crisis of the twelfth century. In line with motives which often determine human actions, once the abuses of the eleventh century were believed to have been corrected by these reforms, the papacy considered that its task had been brought to a successful conclusion. Enough had been accomplished since its main concern had been to strengthen the unity and conformity of views to be expressed by the Curia. Society, however, was not standing still and there was inevitable pressure for further reform. The changes which were taking place in both spiritual and temporal life increasingly demanded a spiritual development from individual Christians and an integral part of this religious crisis was a new ferment in people's lives requiring a new set of solutions and answers. The increase of population, the growth of towns, the increasing numbers of existing specialist functions, namely artisans, lawyers and particularly merchants, the replacement of compact kin-groups by larger, more fluid groups, the lessening of the importance of such rituals as the ordeal, which inclined to the profane superstitious rather than the sacred supernatural, and the crucial shift from acceptance by consensus to a recognition of an obedience to authority, all played their share in formulating the religious crisis with which we are here concerned.

Reacting to the crisis — the *vita apostolica*

From these roots there blossomed an attempt at a new life-style based on a return to the example of Christ and the apostles, a *vita apostolica*, as shown in the events and teaching that took place in Jerusalem and the Holy Land in New Testament times. Thus, in the twelfth century, the time had come for a new encounter between the Gospel and the world. Christ's instruction to search the Scriptures became particularly appropriate. It was strongly felt that in response to this there needed to be witness to the faith, fraternal love, poverty and the example of the Beatitudes. Two texts were particularly stressed: Acts 4: 32 which described the communal life of the first Jerusalem community where the apostles lived fraternally, having all things in common, and Luke 10: 1—12 where Christ expressly ordered his followers to observe poverty as they went out two by two on their mission. Thus the two particular aspects for the *vita apostolica* on which stress was laid were communal living and voluntary poverty but putting them into practice was not so easy. It can be seen from a close examination of the ideas being put forward at the time that three leading principles had come to be developed from this increased reference to and study of the Gospels. The first was an imitation of the primitive Church by the imitation of Christ and his apostles through suffering, spirituality and penance. The second was love for God and for one's neighbour through a literal observance of the Commandments while the third was the attempt to follow Christ's commandment to be perfect, practising a common life of evangelical poverty, manual work and the receiving of alms. A dual response was necessary from the individual Christian which meant that he both returned to the Gospel and yet remained in the world. This had to be a two-fold response and not two separate responses. The Christian's return to the Gospel was to guarantee his presence in the world and it was this presence in the world which was to ensure the effectiveness of the Gospel through a greater awareness of Christ and a deeper appreciation of mankind as one's brother.

An important consequence of this new *vita apostolica* with its emphasis on poverty was later considered to be the preaching of the word of God as an essential way of mission. Preaching became important just before and after the beginning of the twelfth century when it was stressed by such itinerant preachers as Bernard of Tiron (1046—1117), Vitalis of Savigny (d. 1123), Stephen of Muret (*c.* 1045—1124), leader of a group which became the Order of Grandmont, Robert of Arbrissel (*c.* 1060—1117) and Norbert of Xanten (*c.* 1085—1134). By the second half of the century the official church had clearly awakened to its importance. Alan of Lille (*c.* 1128—1203), for example, in a tract written sometime after 1185, placed preaching at the top of his seven-rung ladder of perfection. The official approach to preaching was that it should be reserved to those within the Church qualified to do so and the scriptural injunction 'who shall preach unless he be sent?' was used against those who contravened ecclesiastical decrees in this respect. The problem was intensified when the term 'apostolate' began to take on a deeper meaning involving baptism, mission and preaching, all official activities. Unofficial preaching was usually itinerant, in the vernacular and sprang from the desire of an individual or group to give personal witness to their faith and the way in which that faith should be lived. It demanded a very different response compared with that given to the preaching of bishops, priests and monks. This together with the whole attitude to belief put forward by these individuals and groups bore the seeds of conflict with established authority and represented a real force to which this authority, both Church and monasteries, secular and regular, had to work out a response. The worth of the priest was particularly called into question. Could a priest who lived a worthless life be worthy simply by virtue of the office he held? Did the *ordo*, his position or rank, not need *meritum* as well? The intrinsic merit of the priestly office and the value of sacraments administered by unworthy priests were problems raised again and again by such groups moved by their knowledge of the scriptures.

The *vita apostolica* and its particular application in the twelfth century therefore helped to redefine and formulate the idea of the Christian life and the terms in which it was lived. It could, if so desired, cease to be shaped around the monastic or regular life and it carried with it the implication that monks were not the only ones to be able to find salvation and enter Heaven. There was a new consciousness of what it meant to be a Christian, of what were Christian beliefs and what was the Christian way of life. Ordinary individuals were again to be important and would help to spread the word of God as in apostolic times.

Reacting to the crisis — monasticism

The development of the *vita apostolica* had profound implications for those who pursued the religious life within monasteries. The shift in emphasis away from the view that the only truly communal life could be that led by monks was yeast for the ferment. For many the system of monastic worship was ill-suited to the condition of the new Christian in society and increasingly opposed their cultural development towards more popular forms of prayer and religious observance. Yet for others, monks still set an example of the highest form of religious and contemplative life, the *vita angelica*, that closest to the angels. Their main value to the community was their intercessory function, acting as agents most suited to achieve by prayer a substitution for private penance. Monks existed to perform this vital task and were the most reliable agents through which the penitential debt might be paid and all men saved, but what of really permanent value had the monastic life to offer when face to face with the challenge of the new society where all could follow the *vita apostolica*? Monks claimed that theirs was the truly apostolic life, *vita vere apostolica*, by which they meant that they imitated the primitive life of the first Christian communities which, in a sense, constituted the first monasteries through fraternal lives lived in common. When they entered the monastery they abandoned all private possessions in order to pursue this communal life. The primitive Church had been established in this way by the apostles and thus monks could represent themselves as their authentic successors. Monks alone could claim to achieve the full reality of the Gospel injunctions but although each monk could present himself as personally poor, his individual poverty often contrasted with the increasing institutional wealth of his monastery. If, after 1100, in relation to the arrival of the Cistercians in England, the monastic writer William of Malmesbury (c. 1080–c. 1143) was able to speak of monasticism as 'the surest road to Heaven' this was no longer accepted by many as being so true later in the twelfth century.

Monasticism had assumed such an institutional form for those who lived in common in a temporal regime that it could no longer claim with any accuracy to model itself on the small fraternal Jerusalem community. It was even difficult to follow the Rule of St Benedict. The monk was no longer obliged to live from day to day by the work of his own hands. No longer was it possible, if it had ever been so, to turn the whole world into a monastery and monks usually failed to encounter the realities of the gospel injunction to go out and meet the world. There was, however, deep involvement of the monastic economy itself in secular society as a whole and it was this which brought about what has been termed the 'crisis of cenobitism'. Further, the actual prosperity of individual monasteries brought a sharp contrast with theoretical poverty which should have been the economic and spiritual basis of the common life. Thus the crisis facing monasticism was also the 'crisis of prosperity'.

This enclosed monasticism with its withdrawal from the world accompanied by varying degrees of asceticism, although having a lesser appeal to a society which was increasingly urban and which, at the same time, wished to be increasingly Gospel based, had a paradoxically increased appeal to many. In fact, not only were there more recruits but there were many landowners who endowed monasteries and upon whose families future recruitment depended. These were often as important in monastic expansion as the monks themselves. Although monasticism had neglected the individual in the search for perfection by the imposition of an external routine many monks became more anxious to achieve a deeper, personal religion less hedged about by customary rules. The hitherto essential aspiration of monasticism to seek God by withdrawing from the world had met with criticism from Peter Damian (*c.* 1007–1072) who observed that every faithful Christian was a microcosm of the world as a whole: 'Each of the faithful seems to be as it were a lesser Church'. There were many who were in the world but not necessarily of it, who were no longer prepared to have their religious life lived and preached for them vicariously by monks who lived by a rule or *regula* in enclosed monasteries. There was also a changing attitude to the role of monasticism in education. As monks began to lose their dominant religious role in society, they also began to lose control of and interest in higher education, as demonstrated by the growth of the municipal schools of northern Italy and the cathedral schools of northern France which became the new centres of higher education in the twelfth century. This showed an additional loss of that complete identification with the world, of monasticism as an institution of the Church, which earlier reformers had been so anxious to achieve. Many considered this identification to be no less necessary in weathering the crisis of the twelfth century, Bernard of Clairvaux being perhaps the greatest of these. The new progressive forms of religious life grew up among – and alongside – those of the old. These latter were not to become obsolete and monasticism remained strong because it allowed old and new forms of religious expression to exist side by side in separate houses. While reformers sought a purer Gospel, pilgrims continued to visit the great monastic shrines such as that of St Denis and to consult hermits, recluses and anchorites who, whilst seeking their own salvation, yet served the needs of the society around them. Diverse forms of the *vita apostolica* were channelled

into different religious orders and houses and thus could be
absorbed by society as much as by ecclesiastical authority.

Reacting to the crisis — the secular church

The conditions resulting from this search for the *vita apostolica*
during the twelfth century naturally had consequences for the
Church and its operation in the world. An examination of the relationship between Church and monasteries gives a good indication
of the changes resulting from the Church's reaction to this
religious crisis. The relationship was one between those clergy who
lived in the world *in saecula* wherever they happened to be in the
hierarchy from pope to bishop and priest and those who took vows
as monks and lived according to a rule or *regula* enclosed from the
world *regulariter*.

There had always been a long history of conflict between priests
and monks in the Church and the reforms at the beginning of this
period had particularly insisted that there should be clerical conformity to the standards of purity already expressed in the
monastic life. Celibacy of the clergy was essential for this purpose.
In the twelfth century the condition of the Church demanded an
increased number of priests to administer the sacraments to the
people and to perform the cure of their souls. There began a
recognition of the need for an evangelical missionary campaign
and steps were taken to end what Peter the Chanter (d. 1197) the
Parisian theologian, called its 'most dreadful silence'. To make all
priests monks was obviously not the answer and several of the new
monastic orders then beginning to appear made reference back to
the Rule of St Benedict which emphasized that priests should not
be encouraged to enter monasteries. The Cistercians, for example,
did not have a large proportion of priests joining them. Part of the
answer seems to have been to ordain more and more monks as
priests giving them some pastoral work and yet allowing them to
remain mainly enclosed within their monasteries, although this
did not appear to meet the need for the increased evangelism which
was being demanded. The Cistercians and others continued to hold
out against the admittance of priests and were most reluctant to
ordain a monk. On the other hand the Augustinians were willing to
develop their aims amongst those diocesan clergy, the seculars,
who wished to add to the development of their spiritual life the
benefits and practical advantages of living under a rule. It was

their aim to become canons regular as soon as they possibly could.

As was to be expected, there was much lively discussion on the relative merits of life spent in a monastery and life spent in the world. Religious life should include both contemplation with God and action for Him. The *vita angelica*, that contemplative life led by monks, needed to be reconciled with the *vita apostolica*, that life which Christians should lead when following the example of the gospels. The spiritual awakening in the ferment of the twelfth century gave a considerable appeal to this action as an ascetic battle against vice. It either prepared the way for a subsequent return to contemplation or provided relaxation from the ardour of a time of such contemplation so that serving God in the world became more and more attractive. A mixed life, with the alternation of periods of action which might take the form of ascetic exercises, manual labour or pastoral work in the world, combined with periods of contemplation was seen as a worthwhile compromise in living the monastic life. Of course, the whole debate of the relative merits and worth of the secular and regular clergy brought to the fore the question of the validity and spirituality of the active life. To many it was more difficult to achieve than monastic perfection and was more commendable and meritorious. Gerhoh of Reichersberg (d. 1169) saw the active cleric conquering the world by battle whereas the monk and hermit conquered it by flight.

The results of this discussion were to mean that although meritorious action was still considered to be within the framework of either a monastic or a clerical life or a mixture of the two, a way was being pointed towards the acceptance of the possibility of the laity also being able to lead a spiritual life of secular action. The *vita apostolica* was to be open to all. The activities of the Church as an institution during this period were to a considerable extent overshadowed by the search for the *vita apostolica* which took place amongst its members in the form of the revival of personal piety. Although often personally faced with the dilemma of choice between spirituality or administration, popes and bishops as churchmen mainly concentrated on increasing their efficiency and temporal power and took no leading part in the contemporary crisis of spiritual development and beliefs. There naturally followed a diminution of that sense of the total community of faith

which the Church was expected to provide. There is no saint
among twelfth-century popes.

Reacting to the crisis — the growth of lay piety

In the ferment of the twelfth century the role of the laity was
highly significant. They were the most effective promoters of the
vita apostolica and there followed a proliferation of groups of
laymen and women which proclaimed the absolute and literal
value of the Gospels even at the risk of causing existing institutions to be questioned. All classes were represented in these
groups from nobles and rich men, merchants and traders to those
at the lower margins of society. Those with wealth often sought to
renounce it in the search for evangelical or voluntary poverty.
Students too, in the rapidly growing urban schools, were at the
centre of this ferment. Whatever their condition in society and
wherever they came from, each and every one of these lay men and
women was irrestistibly drawn to express a new life style through
the medium of personal witness. This was done not only by the
way in which they lived but also by spreading the Gospel message
to others. Thus preaching was central to the evangelical awakening. Once people were allowed to hear the gospel in this way a
decline in the religious significance of the clergy followed with an
increasing acceptance of the laity. Indeed the very different social
roles of the people taking part in the reawakening helped in the
acceptance of their religious significance. For example, Jacques de
Vitry (*c.* 1160/70—1240), a contemporary observer and popular
preacher, a regular canon in the diocese of Liège, then bishop of
Acre and cardinal of Tusculum, addressed his *ad status* sermons
across a wide spectrum from rich married people to peasants,
seeing each group as having its own rules and institutions
according to the different types of talents they possessed and
collectively making up the body of the Church under the abbot
Christ. Many of these groups were referred to under the generic
name of the Poor of Christ, *pauperes Christi* and many took on
institutional forms.

These forms of the apostolic movement were very widely diverse
in attitude and activity. Some were special adaptations of the
Christianized feudal institution of knighthood such as the *militia
Christi* of the Knights of the Temple or of the Holy Sepulchre,
the Spanish military orders of Calatrava and Alcantara or the

Portuguese order of Aviz. These were particularly approved of and supported by St Bernard of Clairvaux, taking as they did the Cistercians as their example and fighting the enemies of the faith both within Christendom and at its frontiers. Another example was the fraternity or penitential order based on institutional poverty. This cut across older kin-group solidarities, had no hierarchy of authority, owned few or no material possessions, acted as mutual benefit societies and rejected many of the trappings of ecclesiastical life including, on occasions, the liturgy. Women were not excluded and the example of the beguines of the Low Countries brought a new dimension into Christian life at this time.

Many of these groups of *pauperes Christi* tried to form themselves into numerous orders in the period up to 1215. After that date the pressure was lessened. The founding of the mendicant orders brought together evangelism and the Church as an institution. The study and the preaching of the Bible, the word of God, were henceforth blended within a distinct belief structure, the liturgy of the Church. With the recognition of these mendicant orders the Church hoped to meet the problem of the new apostolic movements which had shunned the traditional forms of the religious life leading to a consequent rejection of the accompanying rules. To these believers the Gospel was the only true rule and St Francis, for example, wished to observe it without gloss, *sine glossa*. None wished to return to the complex legislation of the Benedictines or Augustinians. The *Humiliati* of Lombardy deliberately refrained from drawing up rules to guide their activities. The Church's action in regard to the laity sought to deal with the problem arising from the fact that, here in the twelfth century, the Gospel was regaining its original compelling drive towards the Kingdom of Heaven. This resurgence meant that the spirit was now regarded as being able to work through all Christians whether as individuals or as groups. Such an idea the Church regarded with considerable apprehension. If Christ rather than his Church was to be the way, the truth and the life, what guarantee was there that differing interpretations not laid down by the Church would avoid simple error or even serious heresy?

Reacting to the crisis — the risk of heresy

There was indeed a danger of wrong interpretation as each

individual believer or group of believers went their own way and
each was differently regarded and treated by individual popes on
behalf of the institutional Church. The Gospel which these groups
claimed as stressing poverty and witness and demanding such
things as the avoidance of swearing and oath-taking, often proved
to be spiritual dynamite in practice. As many of these ideas could
be taken to excess the possibility of divergence from orthodoxy
was considerable. This was especially so with the 'formidable and
double-edged inspiration of poverty'. The risk to the Church was
potentially great and often proved to be so in fact. Laymen having
achieved evangelical liberty could abuse it. Once they began to
imitate the Gospels they could also claim that the right to teach
and thus to preach was theirs also. In order to preach the Word in a
truly apostolic way the Scriptures had to be searched. They had to
be spoken about with a broad diffusion of Biblical texts and
translation of at least part of the Bible into the vernacular was
needed. The Church's policy in the case of one pope at least can be
indicated by the reaction of Innocent III in regard to a group of lay
people at Metz in 1199 where he judged that it was a great danger
for simple people to set themselves up as being as wise as learned
authorities when it came to explaining the Scriptures. Although
the idea of the *vita apostolica* needed to be reinforced by the
essential pastoral task of sacred teaching and the spreading of the
Gospel, there was an essential difference between converting
Christians in the times of the Primitive Church and deepening the
faith of those who, by the end of the twelfth century, were regarded
already as Christians. To limit this, the Church's aim was to link
preaching with the hearing of confession and the administration of
penance.

The Church at this time was a compulsory society. In the defini-
tion of heresy and heretics it was the issue of obedience which was
regarded as crucial even though many differences of doctrine and
interpretation existed. Many who witnessed for the *vita apostolica*
were approved by the Church whereas others were condemned. In
the first half of the twelfth century, Norbert of Xanten was an
example of those preachers who were approved and subsequently
found an institutional role whereas Henry of Lausanne and Arnold
of Brescia exemplified those who were condemned and remained
so. In the second half of the twelfth century the Cathars presented
such an insuperable problem that they were totally condemned as
heretics and cast out of the Church. Underlying this issue of

approval by the Church could be found, amongst the proponents of the *vita apostolica*, a conflict between anticlericalism and a willingness to do what the Church wished. This was epitomized in the search for an acceptable distinction between public witness by the faithful who felt enjoined to do so as part of the *vita apostolica* and the functions of preaching and teaching reserved for the clergy. Innocent III saw it as his task to make the distinction clear and so avoid harmful divisions arising. At the end of the century, he established a basic statute embodying this essential distinction which enabled both witnessing and preaching to be carried on side by side by those who were allowed to do so by the Church.

Of course, the increasing use of the Scriptures was bound to lead to varying interpretations, some of which were acceptable to leaders in the Church. One of these was the spread of Millenarianism through the literal interpretation of the Book of the Apocalypse which Innocent III himself may have supported to a certain degree. But unacceptable was the interpretation given by Joachim of Fiore (*c.* 1135—1202) of the way in which the Trinity was worked out separately in history: 'The period of the Old Testament was for God the Father, then with the New Testament came the period of God the Son but now had arrived the period of God the Holy Spirit and the Spirit had to be followed in all things.' He was soon in trouble with the Church.

Those considered to be the most radical heretics of the time, however, were the Cathars (Greek *katharos* pure). The theme of a return to the primitive Church had a considerable appeal to them especially where they could see a confrontation between good and evil. The basis of their vocabulary was entirely Christian; they accepted the New Testament as being divinely inspired; they won recruits through their practice of the *vita apostolica* but as dualists believing in separate worlds, one based on good principles and the other on evil principles which were incapable of coming together, they were different in doctrine from the Christian Church. Although the Church's response to this was mainly one of negative repression, it was led to make positive attempts to put its own house in order and regain from those tempted by Catharism the respect often given to the Cathar leaders for the purity of their lives and the force of their preaching. These Cathars were often referred to as Albigensians because there was a particular concentration of them around the town of Albi in the area of Languedoc in southern France. So serious was their heresy considered to be by the Church that in 1209 the papacy instigated a crusade against them. Attempts by the Cistercians and later by Dominic, who had criticized the Cistercians for their pomp, to combat this heresy both failed in spite of determined attempts by the Church to understand what the heretics wanted. It was to be left to the northern French nobility, possibly for political rather than for religious reasons, to conclude the crusade with the brutal repression of the heretics.

In general however, if there was the danger of heresy to be faced by those seeking the *vita apostolica*, there was also the danger to be met by the Church in the way it was tempted to react to them. Innocent III found the best answer in stressing the paramount need of the time to be the maintenance of the unity of the Church. His view was that certain concessions could be given to these lay groups and to the mendicant orders so long as the unity and authority of the Church at least was accepted by all. Their theological education could be left to another time when the framework within which beliefs were expressed had itself developed to reflect both the spiritual awakening of the *vita apostolica* and the authority of the Church.

Reacting to the crisis — a framework for conformity — liturgy and literature

Although Innocent III concentrated his efforts on maintaining unity with a corresponding recognition of the Church's authority, most clergy were not willing to let theological divergences remain unanswered. The rest of the hierarchy were at pains to have limits defined within which these differing beliefs could be expressed and yet conform to the Church's teaching. The Church had always used the liturgy for this purpose. Liturgy is the way in which Christian society functions when it meets both to propagate its faith and to worship its God, and a Christian's attitude towards liturgy is determined by his view of Christ and Christ's view of him. As the tenets of faith and worship change and develop so liturgy should also change and develop. Historians have long recognized the importance of the liturgy in giving information about the beliefs held at any particular time. Ever since the time of the Fathers, the Church had insisted that liturgical renewal is much more than a matter of new rubrics. Even the most significant material changes in the field of religious belief, such as those of the twelfth century

which included both a fuller use of the Scriptures and a wider
extension of the vernacular, would have remained meaningless
had they not been accompanied by a change in the spirit in which
the liturgy was performed. As liturgy is at the heart of the whole
life of the Church the spiritual renewal taking place with the
coming of the *vita apostolica* had to take place in the liturgical
field as well as elsewhere. This took the form of providing greater
opportunities for private devotion and personal spiritual development with more popular prayers and less restrictive patterns of
misdeeds and penances at the confessional. As was to be expected,
the Church, when undertaking this task of rearranging its
liturgical ritual and documents, took the opportunity to correct
any deviations from conformity which it considered to have come
into existence.

Another difficulty about the liturgy was whether it was to be
regarded as a symbol of piety, where there was a connection
between the liturgy and the mysteries of both faith and redemp-
tion or whether it was to be regarded as a ceremony which would
help along the process of worship. It was to be expected that that
part of the Church exemplified by the pragmatic Innocent III
regarded the liturgy as material for allegorical instruction and not
as something symbolic with the power to represent a mystery only
to the initiated. This debate about the importance of symbolism
also applied to the Bible. For many, symbolism formed an integral
part of biblical (scriptural) interpretation and so continued
patristic tradition. If this was not taken into account in
expounding the Bible there were bound to be theological difficulties. There was thus the need for hierarchical control of what
was read and what was available to be read. This was considered
by many in the Church in the twelfth century to be even more
necessary when those who lived by the *vita apostolica* wanted the
Bible to be used in order to kindle and nourish their faith in a living
God who had manifested himself in history. If the advice of Philip
of Harvengt (d. *c.* 1182) was to be followed, namely 'You have the
means of rekindling your soul', by the repeated reading and
exposition of the Scriptures, particularly if this were to be done in
the vernacular, then the Church would have to ensure the purity of
the liturgy, the control of the literature available, the way in which
they were both used and expounded and by whom such use and
exposition should be carried out. The burning of the books of the
Waldensians of Metz in 1199 may have been a reported exception

to the normal but there must have been considerable temptation to do likewise in other places and at other times. Perhaps the more flexible approach of the Church under Innocent III would eventually have to be replaced by the more rigid methods that came to be used later in the thirteenth century.

2
Hermits, monks and canons

For some hundreds of years after the time of Christ it was to hermits and monks that people had turned to find examples of the lay religious life. It was not the obvious intention of such hermits and monks to provide this example. Their main aim was to attempt to achieve salvation, being close to God in the life of asceticism which they lived and in the rule which they followed and in achieving this, they individually needed to be far away from others. The hermit's eremitic life of individual solitude in the desert represented one way. The cenobitic monk living in a collective community, seeking to lose himself by disappearing, not into the desert but into a community of other monks, was regarded as being just as effective a way of obtaining a formal and segregated type of Christian asceticism. He had no real need for any of his fellow men and in fact, the Fathers had put forward a further maxim, that a monk should, by all means possible, fly from women and bishops in his search for single-minded perfection. There were even examples of monks in this way of life who claimed miraculous ordination by Christ himself and so emphasized that it was possible to be completely removed from the world even when this included the form of the institutionalized church.

Differences between east and west

Although developments in this religious life in the West, referred to today as Western Europe, were not entirely unlike those in the East, the Eastern Mediterranean area, there were often occasions of such varying emphasis that they sometimes appear to have been so. The eremitic ideal as practised by the earliest desert monks of fourth-century Egypt displayed a most radical individualism and competitiveness in the practice of asceticism. This extreme and vigorous behaviour was difficult to institutionalize and the origin of the monk (*monos*), who lives alone, can be traced back to this isolated individualistic asceticism of the hermit seeking his own salvation. The model for the ideal hermit was to be found in St Anthony (c. 251–356) who, motivated according to his biographer Athanasius (c. 296–373) by the Gospel exhortation, 'If thou wilt be perfect, go and sell all that thou hast', fled into the desert at Nitria. Anthony's life demonstrated the need for battles with devils in the solitary combat of the desert. Walled up in a cell he fasted, prayed and fought demons and through his supreme asceticism he became the guide for all future Christians whether by individual or communal emulation.

The different pattern of the communities (*cenobia* from the Greek *koinos*) emphasized this variation between east and west. The east tended towards a mixture of individual isolation and cenobitic or group living whereas in the west there was often a stricter separation of the two. The natural development of monasticism in the east has been depicted as moving from solitude (*eremos*) to community life where the monk, although cut off from the world by living alone in a cell, could practise brotherly love within a monastery and which provided a form of community when needed, for example, for worship on Saturday and Sunday. Although these semi-eremitical colonies would have no formal rule of life, the authority of elder hermits and those who were experiencing the full eremitic life would have been a significant example. The teacher-disciple relationship was widely valued. Instead of a rigid dichotomy between eremitism and cenobitism there existed a spectrum of varying forms of monastic life — from complete solitude to a strict common life — so that the individual could choose that which suited him best. However loose this arrangement, a recognized line of control from Church to cenobitic community was always sought, no matter how much this may have been resisted by those concerned. No really detailed regulation was able to be achieved in spite of the attempts of Pachomius (c. 290–347) at a formal rule when he founded a cenobitic monastery at Tabennisi on the Upper Nile in 315. The dominating tradition was still that a perfect monk had no need for a rule of life. Where a monastic group had developed some form of rule, regulating to a certain extent the behaviour of its own members, no formal link with the Church as a source of legitimacy for these regulations had to be provided.

In the west eremitism and cenobitism often existed side by side. In spite of the eremitic tradition within many cenobitic communities, the way of life of the religious usually took one of these two distinct forms. A monk might make long eremitic retreats between periods of life in the community or he might be a permanent recluse or anchorite (*anachoresis* from the Greek for a displaced person) in some way attached to a monastery and under the control of its abbot. Scores of monasteries were surrounded by small hermitages whose inhabitants were associated with the main community. The growth of stringent control by the Church exercised through a rule was particularly evident in western monasticism. Not only did bishops found monasteries but they also encouraged the adoption of particular rules. So much was this so that eventually the degree of control by the centralized authority of the Church meant that any new monastery was required to submit its rule before it could be officially authorized. Approval by episcopal or even papal authorities would normally require the incorporation of suggested modifications to the rule. This was an important development because, in some cases, asceticism had become so extreme as to raise doubts about its Christian nature. Jerome (*c.* 331—419), Cassian (? main career 404—415) and Benedict of Nursia (traditional dates *c.* 480—543) were not opposed to hermits and anchorites although the danger arising from their excesses in exaggerated and competitive asceticism made Benedict in particular keen to institute a rule which would remove such practices. When this Rule was produced, possibly about the year 530, as a guide for Monte Cassino and other monasteries then existing simply as a collection of independent units, the final chapter went so far as to suggest that he regarded the cenobitic life as a preparation for a more perfect life in solitude. Benedict here appears to show no desire to break with eastern monastic tradition but rather to adapt it to western circumstances. The eremitic life remained an ideal in both eastern and western Christianity although in the west communities became increasingly popular. As there was always the possibility that some of these cenobitic communities would overstress the social group by too much submerging of the self, so that, in the words of a contemporary, like a herd of pigs 'when one grunts, they all grunt' or would encourage the forming of particular friendships, periodic upsurges for a return to a greater concentration on primitive eremitical observance often occurred. Such a desire for a more eremitical approach seems always to have been prevalent at times of change and reform. The end of the eleventh century was one of those periods and there was an increased interest in the early desert model provided by the Egyptian hermits.

Twelfth century spiritual developments — individual

The new religious fervour which had begun at the end of the eleventh century and developed in the twelfth expressed dissatisfaction with the ways in which religious institutions had ossified. They had become concerned more with the form than the spirit. To counteract this, there emerged, particularly in the eleventh century, the desire to express an individual spirituality or private endeavour, undertaken in places remote from the habitations of men. In their return to a consideration of examples from earlier days, men could not fail to know about the religious life which had been practised in the deserts of Egypt and Syria. Many considered that, just as Christ had spent some time in the wilderness before beginning his teaching, the life of prayer and isolation of the hermit could also be used by those who wished to be strengthened for the pastoral life which they would soon enter. Outstanding examples of those who were so strengthened were Vitalis of Savigny, Bernard of Tiron, Robert of Arbrissel and Norbert of Xanten who, in addition to their preaching missions, were later instrumental in the founding of new and reforming modes of religious organization.

Throughout western Europe and above all in Italy, at Vallombrosa, Camaldoli and Fonte Avellana, groups of hermits sought to find a 'desert' to which they could return. They found remote uninhabited places, up mountains, in secluded valleys, on islands and in forests. One such place was Sitria and publicists at the time were not slow to notice the similarity of this name with Nitria, the site of St Anthony's desert. The hermit ideal was thus revived in a world in which its opposite, the communal mode of life, after centuries of growth and development, flourished as never before and it was perhaps an understandable reaction. Throughout the twelfth century this search for life as a hermit developed in three main ways. Firstly, many continued to live as anchorites or to undertake periods of retreat whilst preparing to preach the word of God in villages, in castles and in cities and for the salvation of particular groups who were in need, for example, women and lepers. Like John the Baptist, they wished to take on all the powerful sinners of their day whilst they themselves were maintained on alms. Many of the preachers were like this. Norbert of Xanten, who had attracted large numbers of adherents, both men and women, possessed only what was necessary for each day. He was finally allowed to institute his own community in 1120 in a forest at Prémontré with a number of hermits as followers to whom the Rule of St Augustine was most suitable. Second, some of the hermits found it mutually beneficial to have some relationship with an existing monastery. For example, the effects of this eremitical movement were felt in the monastery of Cluny which not only had its own hermits living nearby, in number about 400 and thus about as many as the monks themselves, but whose abbot, Peter the Venerable (1122—1156), occasionally went into the wooded hills nearby to refresh himself by a brief experience of the eremitic life. Third, the founding of the Carthusians seemed to provide a cenobitic way of life within which the way of life of a hermit could be fully expressed. They set up their monastic communities in the nearest 'desert' available to them, namely high in the Alps at La Grande Chartreuse above Grenoble. There the number of monks was small by contemporary standards. Each house consisted of the apostolic number of 12 with a prior and lay brothers or *conversi*, 16 in number, who both protected them from the distractions of routine work and acted as a buffer against secular society. These Carthusians considered themselves to be combining a form of Benedictine cenobitism with some of the earlier eastern traditions found in the letters of Jerome, in the Rule of St Benedict or in the Scriptures themselves. They rejected many of the monastic features currently in common use, for example, the giving of hospitality. Guigo I (1109—1130), the fifth prior, tried to formalize their views in written constitutions stressing how the Lord went alone to pray in the hills at times during his mission on earth and stating that God revealed his secrets in solitude and silence.

Like Guigo I and Norbert, all hermits were drawn by the example of the desert fathers in seeking to be close to God and to hear his word. They thought that this could not be achieved if they were continually in the midst of tumultuous crowds but the Gospels showed that Christ and the Apostles had spent much of their time amongst such crowds, and so a dilemma faced those hermits who, in the twelfth century, wished to achieve the fullest *vita apostolica*. If they were out of the world, how could they relate to those who considered that Christians should be in the world but not of it? The large majority of those seeking to lead the *vita apostolica* came to the conclusion that it should not be lived out of the world but, whichever way the hermits chose, there were critics

in plenty to disagree. This was perhaps not so much a criticism of
what they sought but rather of the way in which they made the
attempt. Similar criticisms were made against those whose decision led them to live in a community away from the world.

Twelfth century developments — monks and monastic orders

The revived outward-looking spirituality of the *vita apostolica*
was to present to those living in monasteries in the twelfth century
a dilemma similar to that facing hermits. To deal with it they had
to change the situation which had arisen from their recent past and
which owed its basis to the Benedictine Rule with its further
developments at Cluny (909), Brogne (c. 929) and Gorze (c. 933) and
the reforms of the eleventh century. With the increasing search for
a way of achieving the *vita apostolica*, the Benedictine basis and
the contemporary situation at Cluny were criticized by one of the
most important spiritual leaders of the time, namely Bernard of
Clairvaux (c. 1090—1153). These criticisms were to lead to
systematized incursions into the world and formal relationships
with it. These could not be left to the vagaries of individuals or to
groups in single monasteries as this might lead to even more
confusion and error than the original situation. A centralized
organization was needed, recognized by the Church and hierar-
chically governed. Its members were to be bound to the uniformity
of a Rule and its observance and who, whilst moving in the world,
would accept as binding on themselves more exacting moral
injunctions than were proposed for the Church at large. Thus there
came into being for the first time the true idea of an Order, developing from the foundation of the Cistercians in 1098 and evolving
with this centralized authority structure. It was a most distinctive
innovation and perhaps its greatest departure from the Rule of St
Benedict was the formation of a federation of monasteries worked
out in the Charter of Charity (*Carta Caritatis*) with the New
Monastery of Cîteaux (*Cistercium*) at its centre. The real founders
of the Order of Cîteaux may have been those abbots who, in the
General Chapter of 1123, renounced some of their autonomy to a
new corporate body within the Church, so bringing into existence
the first monastic order. Such new orders, which were to be the
main development of the twelfth century, owed much to the
Benedictine Rule and to its development at the important foundation at Cluny.

The Benedictine basis

The Rule of St Benedict of Nursia *c.* 530 and its reformulation and codification in 816–819 by Benedict of Aniane, advisor to Louis the Pious, had represented the most successful and satisfactory answer to the need for a framework for monastic life. The Rule itself was very short and provided in some 12,000 words a remarkably clear statement, easily understandable, about the need for order and discipline in the daily life of monks. It was found to be suitable for communities in widely differing circumstances and though perhaps capable of various interpretations it played its part as one of the central statements of Christian living. The Rule was very clear about the total commitment required from monks and made provision for their detachment from all other potentially conflicting loyalties such as material possessions and attachment to a previous way of life. This formal commitment was expressed in the form of vows. The Rule was designed for autonomous communities of monks but it was also an instrument of control by the Church and specific provision was made for the intervention of the local bishop into the internal affairs of the monastery. The Church, although attracted by monasticism as an incomparable method of renewal of spiritual power, always made it clear that salvation was not to be obtained by monasticism and asceticism alone. The Church and its sacraments were needed. Nevertheless Benedict demanded considerably more obedience from his monks than the wider Church demanded from its clergy or its lay members. He established obedience without delay as the first degree of humility, ordering that the commands of a superior were to be treated as the commands of God and carried out accordingly.

It is important to remember that the Rule was not written by a priest but by a layman dedicated to the search for God. The development of monasticism was a systematization of a more general lay practice which often carried with it a strong anti-sacerdotal tendency. The first evidence of a differentiation between monastic groups and the rest of the membership of the Church occurred when the priestly hierarchy of the Church became institutionalized. As the Church dealt with the new situation caused by Constantine's conversion (312) the monastic movement could be interpreted as a form of protest by the laity against the curtailment of former freedoms and privileges. The importance of this lay status of monks was borne out in the Rule of St Benedict which required that priests should not be let into the monastery too easily and once there, must be made to obey the Rule as did all other monks. They could, however, with the abbot's permission, be allowed to say mass and give blessings.

As the years went by, variations occurred in these autonomous monastic institutions and each generation saw its task as the renewal of the purpose for which monasteries existed. These ideas of regeneration were most often centred on the desire to return to a purer and closer observance of the Rule of St Benedict. This continual reference back to the Rule, no matter what changing circumstances were being faced, emphasized ambiguities in the interpretation of the Rule which had not existed in Benedict's day. The main ideal of spirituality, which monastic reformers always tended to seek in the conditions of their time, had great imprecision surrounding the question of poverty and the difficulty of defining it. If it was clear that the monk who was to be 'poor in spirit' had to root out completely the vice of personal property, what was to be the degree of his 'stripping' and what form could his pure life take at the heart of a community which itself was frequently rich? The term poverty had not been used in the original Rule. Other ambiguities related to manual labour and the position of the abbot. There was also the relationship between the monastic community and judgments made by the local bishop. To submit to such an authority linked the community to the world from which monasticism wished to remove itself and constant attempts were made to resolve this issue. That made in the tenth century at the monastery of Cluny was to lead on eventually to the spiritual developments of monasticism which were to occur in the twelfth century.

Cluny's attempt at reform

The monastery of Cluny was the outstanding one of a system of creations founded in the tenth century as part of the movement of monastic reform to bring immunity from local influences and to return to a more exact imitation of the Rule of St Benedict. The main concern was fighting the local ecclesiastical hierarchy particularly where the bishops and clergy exercised those temporal rights given them by virtue of the positions which they held. The exercise of this temporal power was often so effective that only the strongest of the new foundations such as Cluny itself could follow that part of the Rule which said that monks were not to be subjugated to the yoke of any earthly power. This was interpreted not only to be the secular prince or count but also the bishop and even the representative of the pontiff of the Roman See. Not that all monks wished to do this. Many were most willing to eat meat, often the product of the nobleman's sport, and provide a retreat for such noblemen in their monasteries. The decay of the Rule which had taken place did not bother them. To deal with this sickness Cluny put forward two cures: to escape localism it placed itself directly under the pope and to escape the association with noblemen and their way of life it restored the need for *communitas*. No one was to be allowed in who had not divested himself of private property. The Cluniac principle of *libertas* was based on an all-round immunity from local pressures and exemption from worldly influences. Those monks and laymen who did not agree had to be forced out and this was by no means easy. Odo of Cluny (926—944) had, for example, to order a group of his men to retake the Abbey of Farfa, one of the nodal points of the Cluniac system of related monasteries. One of Cluny's aims in fleeing from the contemporary disordered society was to bring about a situation in which it could meet its religious aspirations.

To break with society in this way and with the monasticism of the previous period, Cluny adopted particular structures based upon the need for stability. It needed to avoid the dangers of hierarchical authority and yet seek to form a new relationship with society which would allow Cluny to participate in it. At first the monks fled from the world to escape the dangers of integration with a society which seemed to them to be completely without order. It was not long before they came back to play an extremely important part in the renewal of monastic piety, the development of a liturgy reflecting this and the christianization of the countryside. They participated in the spread of the contemporary 'Peace Movement' and before long were giving an indication of those changes needed in the papacy and Church hierarchy which were to be brought about at the time of Gregory VII. But by the twelfth century, even if not sooner, Cluny itself was in need of reform. It had become too open to secular influences and the very large numbers of monasteries which it had spawned or which had become affiliated to it, operated independently, not only from each other but also from Cluny. They had all evolved their own internal rules according to their own external circumstances and were tied down under a great weight of custom which came to threaten the observance of the Rule. The chief instigator of this necessary reform was Peter the Venerable, abbot of Cluny (1122–1156). He introduced reforming statutes which, it has been argued, were designed not only to defend the old type of Cluniac monasticism but also to adapt it to the new spirituality of his time. His personal simplicity was a sign of the new religious values of his age and his eremitical retreats showed a concern for the poor and bore witness to his friendship with the Carthusians.

In 1132, 10 years after he became abbot, he introduced many reforms beginning with a reimposition of fasting and silence which many were no longer observing. In so doing he eventually won the support even of St Bernard who in 1152 admitted that Peter had improved Cluniac religious life in many ways. Peter's determination to introduce reforms on succeeding Abbot Pons (1109–1122) stemmed from a movement in papal attitudes to Cluny and growing opprobrium from the Cistercians and certain bishops who were pressing for greater reforms. He met with considerable resistance within Cluny and its associates. The main emphasis of his reforming activity was shown by the collection of varying statutes (in 1146 or 1147) which had been brought into existence up to the time of his death. He justified each one with a reason or *causa* and these *causae* give an exceptional insight into the problems which Cluny faced in the first half of the twelfth century. Previously at Cluny and its other houses monastic life had been regulated by the great customaries of Bernard and Ulrich but custom began to make so many different interpretations that a common set of statutes became necessary. It is difficult to generalize about these statutes since some dealt with the alleviation of excessive harshness and others with the reasserting and raising of standards of strictness but there were some basic themes. For example the statute excluding lay servants from the infirmary showed the new emphasis on the need to separate laymen from monks within the monastery. In the *causa* to statute 23 which dealt with his attempt at a middle course between complete withdrawal and openness to outsiders he said that he wanted to avoid turning the cloister into something like a public street. In the *causa* to statute 53 dealing with the possibility of personal asceticism within the community Peter explained that there was no place except the old church of St Peter at Cluny for the monks to exercise 'certain sacred and secret practices suited to holy men' and so he set aside part of the new church (Cluny III 1088—1121 and the rebuilding of the nave *c.* 1125—1130) where they might pray and mortify themselves as in a hermitage far from the sight of men. These private devotions within the largest church in Christendom were quite distinct from the regular discipline of the community, harsh as even that became under Peter. Statutes 32 and 33 dealt with the practice of charity outside the walls. Charitable distributions at Cluny had been enormous; Peter proposed to restrict these distributions, given in memory of any monks who had died in the previous month, to 50 on any single day. He hoped that this would make the practice of charity less demanding and at the same time avoid any possibility of the growth of a cult of the dead. In the event, however, the urgent requirements of those who were in need meant that the total amount of charity given was in fact increased by Peter. In statute 33 he required all leftovers, some of which had previously been kept and served again, to be given as alms. The purpose of the two statutes appears to have been to inject a more personal and caring spirit of love into the older type of liturgically orientated distribution of alms and services.

An examination of these statutes shows the two broad tendencies to be found in twelfth-century monasticism. These two tendencies were related and were concerned with the reduction of what was considered to be the excessive length of the liturgy. The aim was to simplify the liturgy and yet to increase its significance by allowing greater opportunities for private devotion and personal spiritual development. Peter himself showed that personal spirituality could be increased under the statutes when he personally 'succoured the oppressed, clothed the naked, fed the hungry and secretly founded houses of lepers'. He sometimes so stripped himself to give to others in need as to lack clothes for himself.

In spite of the reforms resulting in these statutes the dialogues between Cluny and others were not to be ended. The most outstanding debates were those with Cîteaux and were exemplified by those between Bernard of Clairvaux and Peter the Venerable. Although there were many instances of agreement, for example, that the Cluniac liturgy was over-long and made the monks 'varicose', there were too many areas of strong disagreement to do other than encourage a divergent form of development. From

Cîteaux therefore came the Cistercians well equipped to meet the religious challenge facing the twelfth century.

The Cistercians — the new 'Pharisees' from Cîteaux

The origins and character of the Cistercians, their relationship with Cluny on the one hand and with the new religious awakening of the late eleventh and twelfth centuries on the other gave rise to problems which were both complex and controversial.

The Cistercians originally sprang from the desire of Robert of Molesme (*c.* 1027—1110) who had previously been a prior in two monasteries and abbot of a third, to leave the prosperous and powerful community at Molesme in Burgundy and with his hermit companions to set up a new monastery at Cîteaux (1098). They aimed that this 'New Monastery' should be more in line with their thinking about the real meaning of the Rule of St Benedict and its exact interpretation. Its site was to be as far removed as possible from secular activities where they could practise a rigorous asceticism. After a year and a half a papal order, obtained by those left at Molesme, persuaded Robert to return there and again take up his post as abbot. It was left to two other exiles, the second and third abbots, Alberic (1099—1109) and Stephen Harding (1109—1133) to continue the developments at Cîteaux. As a basis for these developments the Cistercians eventually went back even further than the Rule of St Benedict in order to justify their actions. They revived the harsher spirit of pre-Benedictine monasticism often invoking the Egyptian or eastern model. One example of this was the individually austere Rule of St Macarius which had no appeal to the Cluniacs, who could not understand its relevance. More importantly the Cistercians began to invoke the 'whole Gospel' as the example for their way of life. This meant that they were to follow Christ in poverty, in simplicity and perfection of life and that this was to become the new model in contrast to the old and as yet unreformed monasticism of Cluny. The Cistercians aimed to concentrate on an evangelical imitation of Christ. That they were able to profess this more easily than to practise it drew from their opponents the derogatory title of the 'new Pharisees'.

At first they were a small, impoverished and struggling community which was boosted in 1112 by the arrival of Bernard and his 29 companions. This not only doubled the size of the existing community but also gave them their greatest propagandist. A considerable expansion ensued. In 1113 Cîteaux sent out her first daughter colony to La Ferté, in 1114 one went to Pontigny, in 1115 another went to Clairvaux where Bernard was made abbot and also to Morimond. The average rate of foundation until 1125 was about one abbey each year and by 1131 an average rate of foundation of 11 each year had been reached. In the period 1125 to 1151 there was a most spectacular growth in which no less than 327 foundations were made and the geographical framework laid. The main Cistercian areas were in parts of France from the Garonne to the Pyrenees, the Loire valley, northward as far as Picardy and in Burgundy on the edge of the Côte d'Or. In England, Yorkshire and Lincolnshire were relatively heavily settled while areas of Wales and the Scottish borders were also colonized. This movement for house foundations then spread to Spain in the wake of the Christian *reconquista* and to both northern and central Italy. Northern, central and eastern Europe with deep penetrations into Poland, Bohemia, Bavaria and Hungary were areas particularly associated with the Cistercians as pioneers. In 1152, the Chapter General called a temporary halt to further foundations but the end of the twelfth century saw a grand total of more than 500 houses.

Without the influence of Bernard it is likely that the number of houses would have been very much less. Indeed the whole history of the Cistercians would have been different. His unique quality was his ability to excite spiritual energy and to set it in motion so that tasks could be successfully completed. Much of the momentum was lost with his death. His life affected the Cistercians in three main ways. In the first place it was really Clairvaux not Cîteaux that was primarily responsible for transforming a small fervent centre of reform into a widespread way of salvation. Cîteaux could thus not remain like La Grande Chartreuse, a way of life for individuals with a very peculiar and strong core. Secondly he was largely responsible for the missionary activities in which the Cistercians became involved. Finally his growing prestige and the astonishing spread of the houses made him a great force in the life of the Church. With a strong and aristocratic temperament he was able to influence both people and events but, as often happens with personalities having such passionate ideals, much of what he accomplished was surrounded by controversy.

It is easier to demonstrate the success of the Cistercians than to explain exactly why it occurred. Doubt has been thrown on the dating of the documents on which the early history of Cîteaux has been almost entirely based. These appear to have been four in number. First, the *Exordium Parvum*, the account of the secession from Molesme and of the early years of Cîteaux to about 1115 and thought to be the work of Stephen Harding with later additions. The second is the list of customs or *consuetudines* for monks and lay brothers and would seem to have been chiefly the work of, or to date from, the abbacy of Alberic. Stephen Harding's *Carta Caritatis* or *Charter of Charity* probably evolved after 1113 and was responsible for the great diffusion of houses. To these documents may be added the *Instituta* or definitions of the Annual General Chapters first codified in 1134. Thus Stephen Harding was considered to be the real organizer of Cistercian monasticism bringing it into the mainstream of monastic development of the late eleventh and twelfth centuries. It is now thought that these early documents of Cistercian history and the institutions which they describe developed over a considerable period of time and possibly do not reflect the exact nature of the order at its beginnings. This research and the doubts which it has raised indicate how very little is known about the origins of Cîteaux. These suggest that it was less well organized and less distinctive than the impression which the Cistercians wished to create later on in the twelfth century so that it could account for the phenomenal success achieved in the first half of the century. Present-day studies of early Cistercian history tend to stress that their development, continuity and interrelationships did not coalesce into such a single and separate movement for the rejection of contemporary monasticism as many have claimed. Instead they reflected a particular form of that search for basic monastic values, with a return to primitive purity, which was so widespread in the twelfth century, occurring as it did in monasteries, in groups and amongst individuals throughout western Christendom. Any originality and uniqueness peculiar to Cîteaux may thus have been exaggerated but there is no doubt that it formed a significant part of that broad movement seeking a return to the sources of the faith and called by French historians *ressourcement*.

Other reasons have to be found to explain why the Cistercians' particular brand of rigour and separation from the world was so successful. Unlike the Cluniacs they were not going to risk any dangers that compromise might bring and this was one further reason for the use of the appellation 'new Pharisees' when referring to them. Jacques de Vitry, in discussing the renewal or *renovatio* of the western Church stressed the utmost importance of the Cistercians. By changing their monks' black habit into grey, they showed themselves eager to reform that which was old and put on (*superaddere*) that which was new. They were willing to do this as the imitators of Christ, following him in poverty and stark simplicity of life, punishing their bodies and rendering themselves his servants. The demands of such a vocation could only be met by those who were mature, strong and dedicated. In an age which stressed the importance of late vocations, the Cistercians could claim to have reversed the Cluniac habit of accepting child oblates by themselves only accepting highly motivated adults into their communities.

The Cistercians — the first new order

It is important to realize that the Cistercians were the first real monastic order in the Church and as such gave considerable direction to its history. Monasticism in its previous Benedictine forms had made no little or provision for relations between monasteries which were in effect autonomous. In the Cistercian Order there was a direct single chain of authority outwards from Cîteaux to additional mother houses as they were in turn established. There was a system of affiliation requiring each mother house to visit their daughter houses regularly. This system of mutual visitation was to check that standards were not falling. For the Order as a whole a supreme legislative body was held at Cîteaux consisting of the triennial General Chapter of all Cistercian abbots. During the twelfth century this system evolved and spread throughout Europe as an effective and united form of organization. Further changes included some element of accountability by allowing for the removal of unworthy abbots by the decision of their monks. This organizational development is chronicled in the Cistercian documents already referred to and was to become the model which the papacy used in allowing the establishment of other orders, including the Benedictines, when they were made to have a system of organization in 1215.

A further reason underlying Cistercian success was their desire to withdraw as far as possible from society, particularly that urban society whose rapid development was a feature of the time. The view of those who regarded towns as being similar to those mentioned in the Old Testament, to Sodom and Gomorrah, found understanding amongst the Cistercians. This attitude meant that at the time of the foundation of the Order at least, they were not in competition with other monks for endowments of churches, for tithes, rents and services. They thus matched the ideal of some proponents of the *vita apostolica* who wished to have the refusal to own tithes as an important element in the programme for monastic reform. Although many attempts were made to reassert the spiritual nature of tithes and to justify their possession by reference back to the Bible there was no doubt that such possession gave a secular emphasis to the character of monks. To many, including the Cistercians, this was thought to be contrary to their imitation of Christ. In carrying out this task of Christian mission in the early period of their expansion and growth, they went to the frontier margins of cultivated Europe to seek and find unwanted lands, from Spain to Poland, from Scotland to the south of France. In renouncing populated areas and their accompanying revenues the Cistercians sincerely believed that they were renouncing the world. The irony was that in an expanding society it was these very frontier lands where the great economic developments of the future were to occur and temptations and difficulties accompanying these were to be faced by the Cistercians as they sought the *vita apostolica*. They attempted changes in their organization, their way of life and their own spiritual basis as these economic changes occurred but in the end they were to be enveloped by them. They had wanted to show contempt for the world and their monastic theology supported this view but this development at the frontiers which was bringing changes in the world was to cause the Cistercians to falter in their aims. It was to be Dominic who would appear to take over the pastoral charge of the new civilization.

One further source of strength to the Cistercian Order was the ability of its organization to tap the enthusiasm of many lay men including peasants who were seeking the *vita apostolica*. The Cistercians were thus able both to lead the layman in his search for salvation and also to have lay helpers in the great tasks facing them in that clearance and colonization which so increased the success of their order. Indeed the institution of lay brothers or *conversi* who were illiterate and labouring half-monks became the essential labour force of the order. These lay helpers or second-class monks were given a strict rule of life as can be seen by the injunctions of the *Carta Caritatis*. By this they were to remain illiterate and were not to expect full monastic status. They were housed at a convenient distance from the monastery and formed a huge unpaid work force. Their numbers increased so spectacularly that in houses such as Rievaulx or Fountains, the *conversi* came to outnumber the full monks, often referred to as choir monks, by as many as two to one and sometimes by as many as three or four to one. An interesting sidelight on such a preponderance of *conversi* was that it led to consequences in the architectural design of Cistercian houses. This was only to be expected because the Cistercians, in common with all monks when designing their houses, always allowed for their theological ideas and corresponding developments in their liturgy to be expressed in architectural terms. The situation in regard to these *conversi* did not remain static nor could it be expected to do so. Although eager at first to be associated with the order, an eagerness which lasted for some considerable time, from 1190 at least, there is evidence that the lay brothers, overworked and underfed, began to dissent and there were no arrangements indicated in the *Carta Caritatis* as to what provision should be made for this. It was not however until the thirteenth century, following ever more increasing dissent, that the whole system of lay brothers was to be called into question.

The Cistercians were aggressive in carrying out their beliefs. The way in which their order developed and the characteristics of its organization meant that they were able to fill the gap between the military on the one hand and the settled and enclosed monastic on the other. Their military attitude to their faith was mirrored not only in the discipline achieved by the regulations in their monasteries but also in their practice of it outside their houses. They represented the frontier guards of faith in both a physical and metaphysical sense. They determined their objectives with absolute rigour and operated to achieve them on both the geographical and spiritual frontiers of orthodoxy. They were ready to attack no matter where these frontiers appeared. Thus they became the leading influence on the Military Orders, the Spanish orders of Calatrava and Alcantara and the Portuguese order of Aviz. The appeal of these 'orders' was to the knightly class converted, as Bernard had put it, from the soldiers of the world *militia mundi* to the soldiers of God *militia Dei*. These orders adopted the Cistercian rule, became affiliated to mother houses and strengthened their links with Cîteaux.

Cistercian missions

This frontier attitude also led to the close alliance between popes and Cistercians. In the course of the twelfth century the Cistercians became the leading crusade agents of the Papacy. Their specific function was 'to evangelize a restive populace and a de-Christianized world' through the mounting of active missionary campaigns. They were mobilized by the papacy to stimulate crusading zeal and many Cistercians played a prominent role in the Second, Third and Fourth Crusades. They were also always ready to embark on an attack on heresy no matter where it appeared. This attack was two-fold, an academic onslaught and a practical operation on both the spiritual and the geographical frontiers of orthodoxy. Their mobilization by the papacy in 1204 against the Cathars was to present them with a severe challenge. To preach and engage in debate with these erudite heretics was one reason why the order which had previously been firmly against education now needed to have in it men of talent who could manipulate words. Hence several troubadours having made their names in secular courts, on being converted, became Cistercian monks. The career of Fulk of Toulouse (d. 1231), troubadour, monk and then bishop, encapsulated the problem facing the Cistercians when missionary and crusading tasks were given them. He entered the order precisely to escape from the world. Yet, far from having renounced it, he found himself thrust into politics because of the political and economic overtones which the order had been forced to acquire in carrying out the tasks it shouldered when it was given the role of the leading crusade agents of the papacy. His career served to demonstrate how closely the Cistercian Order, in spite of its aims and ideals, had become involved with secular society. It no longer represented a means of protest and thus lost much of its appeal to others who were still searching for such. The shift in emphasis following the development of their constitutions had meant a move away from the personal obedience of earlier times, as exemplified by Peter the Venerable at Cluny, to the corporate discipline of the order. This, whilst having tremendous advantages both to the order itself and to the papacy, was no longer applicable to those individuals and groups who were searching for a personal rebirth or *renovatio*, for a personal *vita apostolica* and a personal salvation. Many indeed felt that only the life of a hermit could satisfy this search and found that Prémontré under the guidance of Norbert was to provide them with something they now found lacking at Cîteaux. To many others the religious situation seemed to demand pastoral care, crusading zeal and a stern, ordered and severe personal example, a mixture of motives which the Cistercians, in spite of their earlier brave efforts, were perhaps no longer fitted to carry out as the seeds of decay destroyed their former high ideals. Too much ostentatious pomp accompanied their efforts in the early thirteenth century for them to maintain their earlier success. It is true that the Augustinian canons, priests who wanted to combine these activities with the life of a regular, made a valuable and widespread contribution but the Church of the early thirteenth century was in need of a new order. It was to Dominic and the Dominicans that the Church and the monks were to look.

Canons regular and the Rule of St Augustine

The Cistercians, in addition to attempting to refer back to the Gospels in their search for the *vita apostolica*, were mainly concerned in simply carrying out a reform of, or reaction to, the way the Benedictines as backsliders had followed the Rule of St Benedict. It was because of this that some consider that no lasting reform could have been achieved. At the other end of the spectrum was an attempt at a break with the past undertaken over a much longer period which eventually resulted in a movement to convert all clergy who were not monks into canons living under a rule. The rule under which they were to live was not that of Benedict but that of Augustine.

The development of groups of regular canons who, like Christ, had to live in the world with all its sin and sinners and yet be not of it, stemmed from the papal reform of the late eleventh century. These secular priests who had taken holy orders to work in the world also wished to lead a full common life having the guidance of a rule. Their chief aim was to combine the aspects of secular and regular life, to be both priest and monk. They regarded Augustine as their legislator and Jerome as the teacher of their canonical life and became known as the Augustinian canons, following the Rule of St Augustine. This Rule, not actually composed by Augustine, meant different things to those who wrote and spoke of it and, if it is to be defined at all, three elements are apparent. The first of these is Augustine's Letter 211 giving advice on the common life for a group of religious women and sent to his sister. This rule, known as the *regula sororum*, does not provide a complete guide to the religious life and there is no evidence that it ever served as the exclusive rule for a religious community. The second rule *regula secunda* sets out a programme for the religious life, elements of which had been known and followed in the eighth century whilst the third rule or *regula tertia* is an adaption of Letter 211 for a male community. These rules, and particularly the second and third, were 'rediscovered' in the eleventh century as the canons sought greater precedent and authority from the history of the Church. With their search among the texts, their authority gradually evolved and became registered. One of the most important of these texts was a Bull of Urban II to the Church of Raitenbach in 1092, a 'charter of institutional dualism', which allowed the canonical aspect and the monastic aspect both to be valid and equal forms of the apostolic life. Urban's choice of words was significant. He asserted that canons who had *revived* lost fervour and monks who *maintained* the fervour which they had never lost were both equally faithful to the Holy Spirit.

The more prosperous economic conditions of the twelfth century helped the spread of the canons. They became almost as widespread as the Cistercians and even more so in some areas, particularly in England where perhaps their moderate attitude had a special appeal. The types and size of their foundations were particularly variable. Some were as large and remote as Cistercian houses while others remained minute urban communities of two or three canons. Different groups of them combined canonical and monastic aspects in varying degrees, depending on the emphasis each gave to the *vita apostolica* and also on the demands made upon them by the great growth of towns in this century. The obligation to love and to serve one's neighbour manifested itself through the ideal of care for one's brothers and meant that outward-looking pastoral work was either their own main aim or was being constantly demanded from them by patrons and members of the Church in their areas. Whatever their own inclinations might have been the Augustinians followed Christ's instructions to his disciples to emphasize poverty, simplicity and practical good works. They also took to heart the words of St James that true religion was 'to visit the fatherless and widows in their affliction and keep themselves unspotted from the world'.

They were always ready to respond to the calls being made upon them.

The Rule of St Augustine suited the canons' purposes ideally. It bore the prestigious name of the greatest theologian of the western Church; it seemed highly relevant to the life of the apostles and it was sufficiently vague to allow a host of useful customs to be added to it. The regular canons were thus, perforce by circumstances, led to follow the middle way, striving to maintain moderation and becoming renowned for their judicious and undogmatic temper. Their true religion consisted 'not in what was to be done but in why it was to be done; not in shaven heads but in purified hearts; not in white vestments but in chaste bodies and clean minds'. Much of this attitude was a criticism of the Cistercians whose reform dealt with constitutional problems over and above moral problems and who, despite their undoubted virtues in seeking to convert the world by sheer self-sacrifice within the sanctuary of the monastery, carried an unduly heavy load of Pharisees amongst their number.

Of course to many the moderate regime and imprecise rule of the Augustinians seemed one of those half-hearted spiritual experiments outside the monastery doomed to failure but it had the great merit of appealing to ordinary men who could comply with it and modifications and advancements did take place. Many Augustinian groups were influenced by the Benedictines especially by the value and joy which the Cistercians received from repentance together with the strength and support received from regular observances. Those who attempted this received the support of St Bernard himself. Dominic and the Dominicans were to adapt the generality of the Rule of St Augustine for the development of their own order. The Church and papacy were both able to ensure that not too many of the canons followed their own inclinations and interpretations too freely. At first there was no bond between those not part of the independent congregations, that is, groups of houses at such places as Prémontré, St Victor of Paris and Arrouaise and each house of Augustinian canons was part of the normal secular diocesan machinery. In 1145, a Bull of Pope Eugenius III ordered the canons in Germany to hold annual regular chapters. Many local efforts were made to bring them together especially during the pontificate of Innocent III. Canon XII of the Fourth Lateran Council of 1215 ordered that in every kingdom or province there should be triennial chapters of abbots and priors of all the religious orders and groups which had not hitherto instituted them. The organizational success of the Cistercian 'new order' was to be for the guidance of all. The fact that this Lateran Council also decided that no further new orders should be established indicated both their value and yet the danger of allowing any questioning and searching groups or houses to go their own ways.

The Augustinian or Austin Canons were until recently the most neglected religious order existing in the medieval church. This has meant that the influence they had in providing a vehicle for the pastoral and caring work of the Church in a diocese and a means whereby the laity of the area could feel a response to the Gospels and the teaching of the early Church, has perhaps not previously been given the full attention the order has now been seen to deserve. It was a type of religious vocation which foreshadowed the transition from monks to mendicant friars who were to achieve a much greater harmonization of the life of a secular with the life of a regular.

3
Lay religious movements

One of the most exciting and original elements of the new religious awareness of the twelfth century was the desire on the part of the laity to participate in new forms of religious life and the very real possibilities which came to exist for this participation. Two groups especially stand out, the Waldensians and the Humiliati, both simple Gospel-based movements whose adherents wished to exhort each other to the Christian life and to hear the Gospels. These groups regarded themselves as conforming to the ideals of orthodoxy and did not wish at this period to be regarded as protesting against the Church. It may even be incorrect to regard them as protest movements or to define them as sects but the degree and nature of their deviance seems to place them in that category of heretical movement recently defined as 'artificial rather than real'.

In 1184 both the Waldensians and the Humiliati were included in the decree *ad abolendam* which excommunicated several groups quite indiscriminately on the pretext that they preached illegally, both openly and in secret and that they held erroneous views on the articles of faith and on the sacraments. In fact both the Waldensians and the Humiliati were trying to lead lives according to the *vita apostolica*.

Waldensians — Valdes and the first Waldensians

Valdes, a rich merchant of Lyon, underwent a dramatic conversion in 1173 as a result of hearing the popular story of St Alexis told by a jongleur or wandering player. This tale of extreme renunciation which had by the twelfth century become something of a cult appears to have been an important catalyst in bringing Valdes to voluntary poverty and was the direct impulse to his conversion. The values spread by the Alexis cult went back to the tradition of the *imitatio Christi* and represented an individualistic lay solution to a crisis of conscience rather than that provided by the more usual monastic and institutional way. Those discontented with current social values found a vital message in the *Life of Alexis*. By dramatically changing his way of life, a man could find a personal response to the torments of the age through spiritual renewal.

Valdes's first and personal inspiration was to go and sell everything that he had acquired by usury and to live instead on alms. He next wished to read the Bible for himself, so he went to a local school of theology (*schola*) for consultation on the matter. He commissioned a scribe and a translator to produce a vernacular version of the Gospels, together with some other books of the Bible and some books of the early Church Fathers. His study of the Bible led him to desire voluntary poverty and to adopt a life style which was immediately and radically different from his previous way of life. The Church did not object to those who wanted to live in this apostolic fashion but the question of Valdes's disobedience arose when through his practice of voluntary poverty he and his followers made direct reference to the Bible and began to share their knowledge and experience with others. In other words they began to preach. The issue was further confused because similar life styles were common amongst those sects which, such as the Cathars, had been condemned as heretical.

By 1176, a year of famine in the Lyon region, Valdes had sold all that he possessed, had placed his wife and two daughters in a convent and had begun to live like a wandering preacher. These actions attracted followers so that by 1177 a small community had appeared which by 1179 possessed sufficient adherents to make a tiny delegation to Alexander III at the Third Lateran Council. Valdes and his followers wanted papal recognition and felt that the ban imposed on them by Bishop Guichard of Lyon contradicted the biblical admonition to preach and lead an apostolic life. In Rome their request was passed on to a competent cardinal who then proceeded through the Englishman Walter Map to make a doctrinal examination. This examination produced two results. In the first place Alexander III responded warmly to Valdes's voluntary renunciation of property and gave oral confirmation of his proposed way of life. Secondly he gave oral authorization for him to preach about this life with the strict injunction always to get permission from local parish priests. This represented virtually an unconditional ban since preaching was strictly forbidden to all save those who were specifically ordained or commissioned. Alexander refused to grant them the right to preach unless asked to do so by priests because the Waldensians, although sincere and worthy, were declared to be deficient in their understanding of doctrine. Interestingly, although the right to preach was usually made dependent on theological examination, when Valdes's Biblical translations were submitted to the Curia for inspection they were tested neither for accuracy nor for orthodoxy. Walter Map was scornful of the Waldensians to whom he referred as *idiotae et illiterati* who believed themselves called to preach. They had tampered with scriptural dynamite by using written translations which would continue to exist for use by others. He alleged that their assumption that they had the right to alms was arrogant and criticized them for their lack of Latin and their misinterpretations of the Scriptures. In common with most lay people of the time, many Waldensians were illiterate only in the sense that they could not read Latin.

In 1180 Valdes and his community made a profession of orthodoxy against Catharism. In return they were allowed to preach orally under the auspices of local priests. We know subsequently, in the period 1180 to 1183, that they encountered various difficulties, possibly being accused of anti-clericalism by priests but this cannot be clearly proved. We know too that after the examination of the Waldensians in 1184, attempts were made to have the resulting ban lifted but these all failed. Various splits occurred within the movement and between 1200 and 1205 Valdes himself seemed to have excluded groups in Languedoc and Lombardy. In 1206 or 1207 Valdes died and soon after his death two small groups of Waldensians were reconciled to the Church. The majority, however, were unaffected by this reconciliation and remained disobedient.

Reconciled Waldensians — Durand de Huesca and Bernard Prim

One such group of reconciled Waldensians were the Poor Catholics led by Durand de Huesca. His origins are obscure but it is possible that he was an early companion or disciple of Valdes. He was an educated cleric from Spain or Catalonia who was converted by Bishop Diego of Osma in the great dispute with the Cathars at Pamiers in 1207. He and his followers appear as the elite of the movement and their acceptance into the Church is ultimately linked to the mission of the Cistercians and later that of Diego and Dominic to the Cathars.

They were orthodox preachers of the faith who like others from

1200 had come to realize that they should live like heretics but preach like the Church. They made attempts to win back heretics by word and example *in opere et sermone.* In 1207, following this great debate between orthodox and heretics at Pamiers, Durand de Huesca's group of Waldensian preachers was indeed won over to the Church. The success of this conversion must be seen as part of a wider plan of Innocent III in regard to popular religious movements. The conversion of Durand de Huesca and the Poor Catholics could not have succeeded if there had not already existed a clear prospect of being able to return to the Church and yet still carry on with their work as mendicant preachers. They wished to lead lives of voluntary poverty, preaching within their own community and accepting what was necessary for their daily existence. In 1208 Durand de Huesca and his companions received official confirmation of their proposal about their intended way of life (*propositum conversationis*) from the pope. Their formal recognition by the curia was granted on condition that they were subjected to a test of belief. Thus they received papal approval of their way of life and were allowed to carry on as before but with the express formal recognition of the Church which gave authority to their teaching and preaching.

The Poor Catholics did not constitute a religious order and their movement was probably short-lived but they were of immense significance in that they represented the first attempt by the Church to create some form of organization for a community of mendicant preachers. Their community was a new form of religious organization and its members who were educated and who were almost all literate in Latin, became recognized and orthodox mendicant preachers. The fundamental condition which the Poor Catholics were required to accept was that they should recognize the hierarchy. They had to promise obedience to the pope and to bishops and had to agree to recognize the validity of the sacraments, irrespective of the personal worth of the priest. They also had to agree to receive all the sacraments from the appropriate priests and bishops. They further had to admit that only priests ordained by bishops could administer these sacraments. On these points the Church could make no concessions. But it could still be argued that their implied errors, of criticizing clerics and of taking the sacraments from unordained priests, were precisely those 'Waldensian heresies' which had developed after their ejection from the Church in 1184.

The curia had therefore made significant concessions on the religious life and activities of the Poor Catholics. In the first place, because the Poor Catholics had given up their Waldensian way of life, they were able to continue with ecclesiastical approval. Secondly, they could give up their possessions and property in any form and live on gifts or alms from believers. Thirdly, they could preach freely, could win adherents by preaching and could meet in groups. They were, however, obliged to concede that their right to preach was linked with the specific commission given to them by the pope. They received papal approval to preach as a community without individual members needing permission. Their mission was to preach against heretics and the enemies of the Church whom they were to convert and lead back to orthodoxy. A second type of preaching was that carried out in their own theological schools, where they could preach to their brothers and friends. These 'friends' were probably middle-class 'burgesses' who had placed themselves under the jurisdiction and pastoral care of the Poor Catholics. Such friends could exert considerable influence for in 1209 a group of Waldensians in Milan announced their readiness to return to the Church if their *schola* and its site, which had been destroyed and confiscated by the bishop of Milan, was restored to them. These were probably a group known as the Poor Lombards.

In 1212, a community was formed at Elne near Perpignan by a number of Poor Catholics wishing to lead a penitential life. William, bishop of Elne was ordered by Innocent III to investigate whether Durand de Huesca and his companions named as Durand de Naico and William of St Antoninus were indeed living the penitential life of chastity set out in their *propositum*, whether their tunics were grey or white and whether they still remained under the discipline and visitation of the Poor Catholics. The Archbishops of Narbonne and Tarragona and the bishops of Beziers, Uzès, Nîmes, Carcassonne and Marseille were ordered to protect Durand de Huesca and his special friends until the investigation had been made. The charges against the three apparently included giving sermons which kept many people away from services held by officially ordained clerics. Some of these archbishops and bishops accused Durand de Huesca of having deceived the Church in order to escape punishment.

Innocent III's attitude to this quarrel was most illuminating. He stated that the function of the Church was to set out to distinguish the wicked (*perversi*) from the righteous (*justi*) and that it had therefore a double task of leading the wayward back from heresy and of keeping believers in the true faith. Of the two tasks Innocent regarded the second as the more important. If those who were in error were allowed to sink still further into erroneous belief it would still have been less serious than to alienate the righteous from their beliefs. Innocent warned these critical bishops to be very careful and charitable in their dealings with the Catholic Poor for if they remained orthodox this would be regarded as more of a triumph for the Church than the conversion of any heretics. The Catholic Poor as a group did not expand widely nor indeed exist independently for very long. They pursued a learned mission, caring for souls as well as for bodies at their hospital foundations in Elne, which became a centre for the production of anti-heretical writings.

In 1210, a group of Waldensians in Languedoc, known as *vaudois* and under the leadership of Bernard Prim, undertook to obey papal and episcopal authority and assured Innocent III of this. Bernard Prim and his group of lay penitents promised to defend the Church vigorously against all heretical sects and promised to try to prevent simple believers from becoming hardened heretics. His *propositum* was approved in 1212 and he brought to the service of the Church an apostolate based on exhortation to a life of voluntary poverty and some recourse to manual labour. Prim and his companions had apparently been celebrating the Eucharist themselves in areas in which it was not readily available from orthodox priests. In 1210 it had been conceded that he and his followers had been impelled by honourable motives to do this. The move was regarded as dangerous since it might open the way to a rival Church organization with its own 'pure' sacraments in contrast to those 'impure' ones of sinful priests. Bernard Prim and his followers, while being willing to work with their hands, stressed in their determination to be poor that they would only accept what was necessary for their daily existence.

Heretical Waldensians and their opposition to the Cathars

Durand de Huesca and the Poor Catholics were reconciled to the Church because they believed that the curia would approve their apostolic mission and that they would thus be able to halt the movement towards heresy. Other Waldensians apparently believed that their own hierarchy would be paralysed by the injunction placed upon them to obey local bishops. Instead of coming to terms with the Church they remained independent and drew up a new constitution which preserved the independence of the members. There was to be an annual chapter at which one or two *rectores* would be elected to direct the missionary activity of the community. Secondly, the Waldensians elected ministers from among their members because, as they were excommunicate, they were therefore excluded from the Mass. In spite of this they were not really equal to creating a new hierarchy of their own for their ministers were only nominated for a limited period of service. The implication here is that a central group of Waldensians realized how effective excommunication might be.

So why then were the Waldensians and the Cathars so opposed to each other? The Waldensians had had a long and respectable history of such opposition from at least 1180 when Valdes made his anti-Cathar confession. The struggle against the Cathars was not primarily to be the task of the Waldensians. They were to preach the word amongst the orthodox, in much the same way as Durand de Huesca, Bernard Prim and the other like-minded penitential groups. The Cathars who imitated the apostles in their life-style and who were highly motivated proponents of the *vita apostolica*, attracted by its emphasis on good rather than evil, were, in turn, opposed to the Waldensians. These heretical Waldensians claimed that they could fulfil all the requirements necessary for preaching maintaining that, like the orthodox, they possessed education (*scientia*), had knowledge of the Scriptures and led an exemplary apostolic life. The Cathars used two strong arguments against them. They asserted that the apostolic life led by the Waldensians did not correspond to that described in the New Testament and also maintained that the Waldensians were discredited by their contacts with the orthodox Church. The Waldensians in turn not only criticized them as heretics but also reproached them for taking part in commercial transactions and for owning property.

A fringe group — the lay people of Metz

One of the most extreme groups of Waldensians appeared in 1199 in the city and diocese of Metz. The adherents of this group were *ministeriales*, members of the lesser nobility in the service of the empire. In 1199, this group of lay men and women were accused of reading from a French translation of the Scriptures which they had made and also of disobedience to the bishop of Metz. In addition to their vernacular translations of the gospels we know that they possessed the letters of St Paul, the *Moralia in Job* of Gregory the Great and 'many other books' in French.

Innocent III's attitude towards them was similar to that of Alexander III towards Valdes. He approved of their desire to understand the Scriptures and by appreciating their *scientia* acknowledged that they were not entirely uninformed yet he pointed out the depth of meaning in these texts which not even learned doctors of the Church could fully understand. He stressed the profound nature of the Holy Scriptures and compared the group to babies capable of digesting only milk and not solid food. He recommended to them that they needed only to know 'of Jesus Christ and him crucified' as the simplest yet deepest tenet of Christian belief. He further emphasized that the Church possessed doctors specially charged with preaching whose function the laity had no right to usurp. Although he disapproved of their conventicles and ideas on the priesthood, which tended towards the Donatist position of lack of confidence in priests, Innocent sensed that to act peremptorily might weaken the faith of these simple people. He therefore refused to judge them before he possessed all the facts of the case as he could not tell whether the matter centred on a slight error in faith or on notorious doctrinal differences. The bishop of Metz was instructed to inquire into the authorship and intention of the biblical translations, the beliefs of those reading them and their teachings. Finally he was to ask whether due respect was being shown both for the pope and for the Church. The bishop reported the continued disobedience of the Metz sectaries but Innocent still felt that he possessed insufficient evidence and turned to a commission for advice. This commission composed of three Cistercian abbots of Cîteaux, La Crête and Morimond declared the writings heretical and apparently the books were burned. This group in Metz was very much on the fringe of what was and what was not permissible in the view of the Church. Presumably the group was stamped out as nothing more was heard of them after 1199.

Humiliati

Whilst Burchard of Ursperg (*c.* 1210—1220) saw the Humiliati as the forerunners of the Dominicans because of their preaching activities and accused them of acting without authorization or approval when 'thrusting their sickle into the harvest of others', the Humiliati in fact had received papal approval of their way of life in 1201. They were unique in offering a choice of the religious life to their adherents, both male and female. They could either live in conventual communities under a type of rule or alternatively they could remain as laymen and women, practising a limited form of voluntary poverty within the framework of the movement and within their own family groups.

The Humiliati were located mainly in Lombardy and seem to have come from the upper levels of society. They too, like the Waldensians, were anathematized in 1184 along with a whole group of heretics and like the Waldensians their only apparent error was their failure to observe the proscription on lay preaching rather than the teaching of false doctrines. In this preaching they concentrated on their own experience of the Christian life. In 1199 two leading members of the group, James de Rondineto and Lanfranc de Lodi came to the Pope to seek approval and recognition of this way of life. Innocent declared himself unable to grant their request without deep thought and considerable investigation. As the character of their life was different from that followed by any existing religious community, it required special consideration for it contained lay, clerical and monastic elements. There was at least one earlier precedent for this. In 1091, that same Urban II who had declared it his belief that the Holy Spirit was inspiring the reform of the regular canons also observed that the communal life of lay people was modelled according to the form of the primitive Church. Bernold of Constance who reported the Bull which contained this statement described the innumerable multitudes of converts to this primitive life and placed them in three categories, both men and women who had vowed obedience, celibacy and poverty in separate communal lives, and married couples who lived according to strict religious principles.

The original and strongest branch of the Humiliati was composed of lay people who lived in their family groups practising strict evangelical precepts in their daily lives. One such precept, based on the Epistle of St James, caused them to reject oath-taking, 'letting their yea be yea and their nay be nay'. In the Church at that time, it was only clerics who were considered sufficiently worthy not to have to swear. Jacques de Vitry observed the Humiliati in 1216 when he travelled through Lombardy and admired them as almost the only orthodox group in the heretical city of Milan. The Chronicler of Laon *c.* 1220 emphasized the importance of family life, prayer, preaching and mutual support in the life of this group. Humbert de Romans praised their austere life style, their simple dress and quiet domesticity, considering them to be aptly named because of this humble life of manual work. This lay group had as its framework the fraternity, an organization which by providing mutual aid and benefits in an atmosphere of piety corresponded to the exigencies and uncertainties of urban life. The sick and dying were to be cared for and elaborate arrangements were made for funerals. Simple rituals were prescribed such as the saying of the Lord's Prayer together or observing the seven canonical hours of prayer in an informal way. This group was known as the Third Order or as Tertiaries.

The First and Second Orders of the Humiliati were composed of priests and unmarried lay people, both men and women, who lived separate and ascetic lives in religious communities according to a form of rule at first unrecognized by authority. The problem which the Humiliati posed for Innocent III was considerable. Whilst it might have been relatively easy to have regulated the Canonical First Order and the Conventual Second Order and to have drawn them into the Church like existing clerical and regular groups, it was particularly difficult to organize lay people who wished to lead apostolic lives in family groups on the model of the early Church and who had already been anathematized. So Innocent III initiated what was to become a recognizable feature of his pontificate whenever he encountered a religious group about which he was unsure. He asked the leaders of the Humiliati to present *proposita* or short statements indicating their willingness to devote themselves to lives of Christian piety. A special commission representing those qualified to comment on each of the three Orders, composed of a regular canon from the community of Mortara, two Cistercian abbots of Lodi and Cerreto and the Bishop of Vercelli, was established to receive, examine and pronounce authoritatively on these *proposita*.

As a result of the findings of this commission in June 1201, the First Order of Humiliati was specifically recognized as a religious community with obligations and privileges set out in its *ordo canonicus*. The Second Order had its monastic way of life approved by the *institutio regularis* which conceded to these unmarried lay men and women the status of *religiosi*. Both these orders were to be regarded as regular communities with endowments and corporate possessions and even, in the case of the First Order, exemption from tithes. The Third Order of married lay people received papal approval of their way of life but could never, of course, be accepted into the Church as *religiosi*. Innocent's instructions to this group of relatively aristocratic lay people, apart from enjoining them to remain together in family groups, were largely concerned to indicate how they might avoid excesses. They were to eat only two meals a day and those sparingly. They were to fast twice a week unless weak or ill. They were to give all excess wealth to the poor. They were to avoid all forms of usury and were to return any gains made in this unlawful way. They were not to wear ostentatious finery. The form of voluntary poverty thus practised by the Humiliati involved considerable personal restraint, representing as it did a way of life more austere and demanding than that of the ordinary layman, yet at the same time avoiding the severity of monasticism.

There was a strong noble or urban patriciate element in the movement which involved leading Lombard families such as that of Porta Orientalis and Jacques de Vitry claimed that almost all of the Humiliati were literate in the sense that they could read Latin. They could not have known the primary demands of the Gospels unless they were able to read for themselves nor could they have understood the *vita apostolica* simply by being told about it. We know that they, like the Waldensians, organized *scholae* to offer training in preaching and in teaching and in order to be able to refute error they must have had a thorough knowledge of scriptural texts.

The most notable privilege granted to the Third Order of Humiliati by the Pope was the extraordinarily liberal permission to preach. Every Sunday at some suitable place those Humiliati 'wise in faith and expert in religion' might preach as long as they ignored theological questions and dealt only with exhortations to the Christian life. This authorization to preach was in direct contravention to the fierce legislation of the twelfth century with its stress on preaching only 'when sent' and was in its way unique. Although a bishop's licence was still necessary before a layman could preach, Innocent expressly commanded the bishops not to refuse. Jacques de Vitry painted a vivid picture of the contribution of the Humiliati. He was convinced of their opposition to heresy and described how in squares, open spaces and in secular churches they 'prudently convinced the impious from Holy Scripture and publicly confounded them'. He believed that they alone in 1216 were holding back the threat of heresy in Milan.

There were of course many other laymen and women who also felt the call of Christ and were moved by the Holy Spirit towards the *vita apostolica* but by no means so far as the Waldensians and the Humiliati. These Christians tended to make demands on the Church, its clergy, monks and regular canons and indeed upon those in lay groups who could help them in their religious aspirations. Most of the demands made were upon the Church and its clergy and it was in one tradition of the Church that the most persistent of these demands came from women.

4
The friars

In his *Historia Occidentalis* or History of Western Christendom (*c.* 1220) Jacques de Vitry, preacher, canon regular, bishop and observer of the contemporary religious scene, wrote about the Franciscans as the quadripartite foundation which the Lord had added to the religious institutions of the Church to join the hermits, monks and canons. Not only had they added a new rule but they also represented a renewal of the old in the state and order of the primitive Church. He wrote of them enthusiastically as the 'new athletes', he described their religion as truly that of the crucified poor and he referred to them as an order of preachers.

We have seen how for monks in the twelfth century the idea of the *vita apostolica* meant a common life of personal poverty and prayer and how in that twelfth century the view of life lived by the apostles in Jerusalem was interpreted in purely monastic terms without any commitment to engage in proselytism or pastoral work. This view of the *vita apostolica* was gradually reinterpreted by monks or differently interpreted by canons so as to include at least some pastoral work and finally emerged after 1215 as the ideal of the mendicants, the Friars Minor or Franciscans and the Friars Preachers or Dominicans, who found in the apostolic life of the New Testament the example for their own communities of poor itinerant preachers. The ideal of both these mendicant orders was a life which combined evangelical poverty, charitable love and wandering proselytism in the world. They represented a gradual evolution in spirituality, a turning away from a purely ascetic ideal of Christian perfection towards a new devotion to the humanity of Christ. The ideal of imitating the apostles and saints was replaced by the ideal of the imitation of Christ himself which Francis and the early friars epitomized. This ideal cut across and incorporated many traditional monastic values by its unique combination of action and contemplation, stability and peregrination, eremitism and cenobitism. It offered to adherents a new vision of a life in, but not of, the world and which was open alike not only to monks and clerics but now also to laymen.

Burchard of Ursperg, a German Premonstratensian canon writing *c.* 1210–1216, displayed great perception in his comments on the Franciscans and the Dominicans whom he linked respectively with the Waldensian groups of Poor Catholics and the Humiliati. We have seen how papal attitudes to both these groups had already made possible a place within the Church for groups of wandering preachers who lived by begging and this in spite of the difficulties caused with the hierarchy. As both orders of friars developed it can be seen that they owed much to others. The Dominicans, many of whom like Dominic himself, with a strong urge to preach and an even stronger urge to obey their superiors, took the Rule of St Augustine to which they were already professed as the basis for their movement and added customs to it. The Franciscans, although a completely new order, were in some ways heirs to the Cistercians in their piety and in their devotion to the person of Jesus Christ and to the Humiliati in the way in which every walk of life could be embraced in the movement with its First Order of celibate friars, the Second Order of enclosed nuns and the Third Order or Tertiaries of married people living according to a simple way of life.

The Franciscans

Francis (1181/2–1226) had come to Innocent III in 1210 seeking approval for his way of life yet unwilling to accept a traditional rule. In the face of considerable hostility from the hierarchy Innocent had to determine how this group from Assisi might be incorporated into the Church. Ought similar concessions to those already granted to the Waldensians and Humiliati be made or ought the community to be forced into an institutionalized form and thus face the risk that by conforming it would lose its originality? Innocent had seen just how fateful the rejection and ban of 1184 had been on these other groups but even so his measures towards Francis and his companions were to some extent temporary. Innocent did not decide immediately. At first he allowed the new community to remain in existence and decided to watch its development in the course of the next decade. The reserve of the curia in this matter is understandable. Francis had already won the support of bishop Guido of Assisi through whom he gained access to Cardinal John Colonna whose intervention and high-status authority was to prove vital. Objections from other cardinals were answered by representing Francis as the norm of evangelical perfection *perfectio evangelica* and it was in this form that his movement was first recognized.

Innocent allowed the movement to continue on two conditions. The first was that he and his companions were to be tonsured so that as clerics they could then be given oral permission to preach anywhere, the *licentia praedicandi ubique*. The second and vital condition regulated the question of leadership to the satisfaction of the curia when Francis promised to be 'in all things obedient to the Holy See' and his companions promised obedience to him. Thus the arrival of Francis at the curia had forced Innocent to formulate his attitude to a movement which, like others, was developing in response to the spiritual needs of the time but which, unlike the Waldensians and Humiliati, had not been accused of disobedience. Whereas in the case of these more developed movements, he had asked for evidence in the form of *proposita* and had called upon outside advice, Innocent decided to wait and see what form the new community might take.

'Let us be like Christ' — the ideals of Francis

In his way of life and that of his followers, Francis wished to reincarnate the life of Christ and the apostles updated to the early thirteenth century. He was dedicated to the ideals of poverty in Christ's Gospel injunctions, especially to the account of the sending of the Seventy. His way of living was extraordinarily hard, far harder indeed to bear than the way of life of the most ascetic monastic orders including even the Carthusians, for Francis, aimed to renounce not only all individual but also all common property thus depriving his followers of even the normal collective security of the cenobitic community. Further, Francis intended that this extraordinarily harsh standard of poverty should be combined by his followers with a serving and ministering activity in the world. Even from the earliest days of the order these two objectives were to conflict with each other. Yet it was precisely from this combination of harsh poverty and ministering activity that the Franciscans drew their greatest spiritual force and ultimately helped to recruit such huge numbers that the original movement became faced with considerable strains.

Within a few years of Francis's death and even amongst those
who had been closest to him, opinions differed strongly as to the
original ideals of the founder of the Order, of its original structure
and purpose and of the correct interpretation of the Rule. Had
Francis really sought to form an order in the canonical sense, an
order of preachers or a cloistered community? Had he intended to
found a group of lay Tertiaries like the Humiliati which under
papal direction subsequently crystallized into specific orders of
men and women? Or did Francis simply wish for the renewal of the
Christian life, following an updated example of the apostles, a
movement which was then taken over by the hierarchy, channelled
into an order and subordinated to the plans of the curia? Such
problems can only be solved by examining the organization of the
Franciscans in their earliest years.

Jacques de Vitry described the movement at an early and
unformed stage in its development. In 1216, on his way to Perugia
to see Innocent III on behalf of the holy women of the Liège area,
he encountered the first Franciscans whom he described as
formerly rich and worldly, both men and women who, having given
up all for Christ's sake and fled the world, were now greatly
esteemed by pope and cardinals alike. They alone were a consola-
tion in a time of worldliness and litigation from which all talk of
things spiritual had been driven. In the daytime the men went to
preach and do good works in the towns and villages; by night they
returned to the hermitage or solitary place. The women lived near
the towns in hospices accepting nothing but living by manual
work. They were greatly disturbed that they were more honoured
than they would have wished by laymen and clerics alike. Jacques
de Vitry highlighted the annual gatherings of these first friars at
which they dined and prayed in common. After this they dispersed
for the rest of the year throughout Lombardy, Tuscany, Apulia
and Sicily. 'I believe,' he said, 'that out of hatred of the bishops
who are like dumb dogs who don't know how to bark, the Lord
wishes to save many souls through these simple and poor men
before the end of the world'. This account is invaluable since it
provides information about the friars before the development of a
formal structure and comes from a reliable and well-informed
contemporary observer.

In the search for evidence from the earliest years of the
Franciscan order it is not always easy to separate Francis's ideas
from those of his biographers. Almost all the Franciscan sources

appear to be coloured by the later controversies within the order and we must approach the evidence with caution, starting from his first rule. In a dramatic and theatrical gesture he stripped himself of his clothing and all symbols of his social status so that 'naked he might follow the naked Christ'. As a 'new man' and with an adopted family of substitute 'brothers' which numbered eight, Francis divided them in apostolic manner into four sets of two and sent them out like the apostles to preach. When they reached the apostolic number of twelve Francis composed a brief rule consisting mainly of passages from the Gospels. It was this, the so-called *Regula Primitiva* of 1210, which Innocent had been so concerned to have set down. A rule, however simple, was necessary. From what can be pieced together of the *Regula Primitiva* it can be seen that the earliest Franciscans were allowed to supplement what food they could earn by manual labour in leper houses and other places by a life of begging amongst the poor. They were not to use self-defence in case of attack by those hostile to them. They were to walk everywhere, only riding on horses in the utmost necessity. Here was a conscious imitation of the apostles who had gone barefooted and who only rode on donkeys. Again Jacques de Vitry witnessed the success of the movement for, 'by God's grace, they have had great success and have made many conquests in such a way that one who hears the call, in turn calls others'.

As the Franciscans already lived by an orally approved rule, they do not seem to have met with difficulties over the decree of the Fourth Lateran Council of 1215 against new rules and new orders. Or indeed if they did, these difficulties were overcome by the support of the pope himself against the conservative bishops and abbots of the older orders and groups. The Franciscans made so many recruits that, in their General Chapter of 1217, the decision was made to establish outposts of their community for the first time outside Italy. The order was divided into provinces, six in Italy, two in France, one each in Germany, Spain and the Holy Land. It soon became clear that the original rule, the *Regula Primitiva*, was inadequate for a growing international order and so another rule, the *Regula Prima*, really the second rule, was composed by Francis who had been prevailed upon to make these alterations when he returned from the east. The *Regula Prima* differed from the *Regula Primitiva* in that the whole emphasis of the 23 chapters was towards a more regular life style with a hierarchy of officials, a novitiate and a more organized reception of

candidates to the order. In 1223, this rule, with a number of significant modifications, was accepted by Pope Honorius III as the
definitive rule of the order, the *Regula Bullata*.

The institutional expansion of the friars was both rapid and
successful yet there were many problems and difficulties too. In
the early days the convents of the friars were not places where
stable communities were based but temporary transit camps from
which a group of friars might carry out an active apostolate. Far
from being real settlements these 'convents' reflected the idea of
the hermitage with some form of temporary shelter in a cave or
simple hut. Francis had urged his followers to live in the world as
pilgrims and strangers precisely so that they would not become
attached to any one place. They entirely avoided the Benedictine
notion of stability having absorbed into their idea of the apostolate something of the extensive travel in which the early apostles
were engaged. The institutional expansion of the group thus posed
considerable problems and we know from Jacques de Vitry that
the lack of careful preparation by the friars threatened their
missionary endeavour. In 1219 60 brothers set out for Germany
ignorant of the language yet hopeful of some miraculous means of
communication. Not surprisingly the mission failed, not to be re-
established for another two years while the friars themselves were
taken for heretics. By 1220 Jacques de Vitry was openly more
critical of this lack of preparation because of the danger to the
movement of sending out into the world not only mature religious
(*perfecti*) but also young people without training who needed a
period of testing and convent discipline.

The Franciscan Order

The ideals of St Francis should always be separated from the
reality of the Franciscan Order. If Francis was indeed the founder
of an order, he was a highly reluctant founder. Religious orders
require organization, administration and the possession of goods
and permanent housing and these features were alien to Francis.
By 1220 the development of the order had been taken out of his
hands and by 1260, had he been still alive and starting afresh as a
layman, he would not have been allowed into the order. Three
cardinal features of Francis's message were poverty, lack of
interest in education and essential non-clericalism. By 1260, the
Franciscans were primarily an educated clerical order enjoying the

use of possessions without actually owning them and were deeply involved in the universities. The Franciscan order underwent a great change in the course of the first half of the thirteenth century when it became torn in two factions, the Spirituals and the Conventuals. The ideals of St Francis were pursued by the Spirituals whereas the realities of a contemporary religious order were accepted by the Conventuals.

Modifications to the Rule began to occur within Francis's own lifetime and the process accelerated after his death. The majority of these modifications appear to have been introduced to help the order carry out its preaching function more effectively. The establishment of settled communities, the relaxation of the ideal of poverty and the cultivation of the Franciscans as an academic order were all designed to help student friars who, it was hoped, would become effective preachers leading the laity to a more active and spiritually satisfying experience of Christianity. Although poverty was the central feature of St Francis's ideal it was never the only feature and he genuinely wished to convert the laity to a more perfect way of life. Thus, although he would probably have disapproved of the later modifications, he would no doubt have understood the motives behind them. The Spiritual Franciscans attempted to revive the observance of the Rule in its purest form and would perhaps have seen themselves as St Francis's most faithful followers. However, their attitude to authority and, in particular, to the pope was completely alien to the obedience which St Francis expected of his friars.

Francis is perhaps best seen as an isolated figure rather than as the founder of the order which bore his name. He may have provided the original inspiration but the movement soon became a victim of thirteenth-century circumstances and was radically altered. The original character and message of Francis made him extraordinarily difficult either to follow or to forget. He could not be followed because of his unique approach, nor could he be forgotten since he was the whole inspiration behind the founding of the Franciscan Order. A townsman himself, it was natural that Francis's message would be acceptable to the people of the developing towns of the time, enabling them to find an apostolic satisfaction for their spiritual needs.

Dominicans

Burchard of Ursperg, who had seen such similarities between the Waldensians and the Franciscans, also claimed that the appropriate and rightful successors to the Humiliati were the Dominicans, followers of Dominic of Caleruega (*c.* 1172–1221) who became members of the Order of Preachers. We have therefore not only to consider the validity of Burchard's judgement but also to ask why the Dominicans and the Franciscans were different. Both Francis and Dominic came from environments in which heretical elements were strong. Assisi was governed by a *podestà* who was a Cathar, while in Languedoc Dominic was at the centre of a Cathar region. Yet the conscious reactions of each were totally different. Francis had been through a personal crisis as a result of which he saw himself called to a particular way of life by Christ himself. Others could join him if they so wished and had been called in a like way. On the other hand Dominic felt the call both to fight heresy on behalf of the true religion and also to lead others in doing so. There were also local influences which brought about similarities in the sophisticated representative structure of the Dominican Constitutions and the *cortes* or representative assembly of Castile.

Dominic and Fulk of Toulouse

Dominic's first known encounter with heretics was in 1203 when as an Augustinian canon on a diplomatic mission he passed through Languedoc. Later, in 1204 and with his bishop, Diego of Osma, he met the Cistercian mission to that region in Montpellier. This mission led by Arnold Amaury, Abbot of Cîteaux, Peter of Castelnau (d. 1208) and Raoul de Fontefroide has been regarded as a failure because it apparently achieved few results. This may well be too severe a criticism. We know that Innocent III wrote frequently to the Cistercians about the superior merits of the active life and stressed the need to sacrifice some of the joys of contemplation in order to carry out this evangelical task. Innocent had already advised his agents not to do or say anything which might compromise their work urging that they should be careful to give the heretics no cause for criticism of either their words or their actions. In Montpellier the Cistercians lamented their lack of success with the heretics and appealed to Diego for advice. Their problem was the scandalous behaviour of the clergy which they did not feel able to correct — particularly since this would take valuable time from their preaching. Diego advised that they should leave the clergy and throw themselves even more emphatically into their preaching. They should attempt to imitate Christ and his apostles, shun gold and silver, travel on foot not horseback and be humble in all aspects of their life. Such advice was by no means unique. It was in face almost precisely what Valdes, Durand de Huesca and Bernard Prim had attempted or were attempting in those same areas. The advice perhaps tells us much about the nature of the Cistercian mission for quite clearly the Cistercians had been using horses, wearing rich clothes and were appearing as lavish spenders, all of which must have served to cut them off from local communities. Apparently they thought that they were doing their best and indeed, to be fair to them, the task was seemingly impossible. After all, how were heretics to be won over and the Church regenerated? Diego's offer of help was received with alacrity and at first he worked with 12 Cistercian abbots proclaiming the faith while living in voluntary poverty. In a letter of November 1206 Innocent III wrote to the Cistercians asking for an expansion of the apostolic mission so that they could fight the heretics by word and deed *in opere et sermone* by putting on wretched clothing so that both by teaching and by example heretics might be recalled from error.

At this critical moment in the history of voluntary poverty in western Christendom this new mission was by no means unique. Diego and Innocent III both had experience of organizing groups of itinerant preachers who lived in absolute poverty in imitation of Christ and the apostles. Innocent had already encountered not only Humiliati but also Waldensians and Diego had dealt with both Waldensians and with Cathars. In 1207, a series of meetings and organized disputations were held at Pamiers and Montreal bringing together orthodox preachers in debate with Cathars and Waldensians and as a result some conversions were made. The most notable of these conversions were those of Durand de Huesca and his Poor Catholics but these may have been carefully arranged beforehand following negotiations with the curia on the understanding that the Poor Catholics would be allowed within the Church as wandering preachers with all that that implied.

The problem still remained of how to convert Cathars and it seems that Dominic had begun to concentrate on finding a lasting means to this end. In 1206 he had founded a religious house at

Prouille in the diocese of Toulouse in the Cathar heartland. At first he attracted to Prouille the daughters of the impoverished lesser nobility, whose education and upbringing were likely to be entrusted to the Cathars, trying to inculcate them with orthodox ideas and to create a new form of religious life for them. The older aristocratic women, often themselves former heretics, came to satisfy their demands for a life style of such austerity that previously Catharism alone had offered in that area. The community at Prouille became vital to the preaching mission as an outpost at which preachers could rest between missions in much the same way as the Cathar resting places which catered for the *perfecti* or priests of that religion and which were also usually run by women. The community at Prouille developed from being a sort of reformatory for delinquent Cathar girls into being a serious and vital centre of missionary endeavour in which women played a crucial role.

The principal benefactor of Prouille was Fulk, bishop of Toulouse, friend of Jacques de Vitry, who shared his interest in women's communities and who saw their value in the struggle against heresy. In 1215 Prouille was taken into papal protection and when the Order of Preachers was established Prouille became its property. For the period from the death of Diego in 1209 to 1214 we have only the evidence of Jordan of Saxony, Dominic's first biographer, for the details of his career but it is evident that Prouille continued to receive benefactions.

In 1215, Fulk gave Dominic the special charge of organizing and leading a group of diocesan preachers. The charge went beyond papal policy as it had so far emerged for it not only specified that the men should go about on foot preaching the word of God in evangelical poverty but it also took the first step to ensure that the preachers would not be beggars. The charter from Fulk which allowed Dominic and his followers to preach in the diocese of Toulouse gave that portion from the tithe revenues of parish churches normally reserved for the support of the poor to these brothers who had chosen to live in evangelical poverty. In 1215, at the time of the Lateran Council, Fulk and Dominic were together in Rome to seek approval for their charter and confirmation of their revenues. The confirmation of their revenues caused little difficulty but the problem of the official approval was a different matter. They could not be approved as a new order within the Church since Canon XIII of the Council expressly forbade the formation of new religious groups or orders. Innocent therefore advised them to return and consult amongst themselves about the order they would join. They chose the Rule of St Augustine, the rule which Dominic already served and which could be expanded to form the basis for the new community. They were able to add a set of ascetic practices from the customs of Prémontré on the one hand and on the other, they were able to allow the acceptance or holding of landed property if their churches stood on it. They were also able to accept the security of revenues. Fulk and his chapter granted them three churches and in one of them, Saint-Romain in Toulouse, Dominic and 15 companions established themselves with individual cells for sleeping and studying and a cloister. In short, they had become friars. Dominic sought approval for his new organization and received it from Honorius III at the end of 1216. Honorius addressed them first as the prior and brothers of Saint-Romain, preaching in the Toulouse region but by 1218 their special instruction to preach had led him to call them the brothers of the Order of Preachers.

Unexpectedly in 1217, Dominic suddenly announced that all the brothers were to leave Toulouse to go out into the world. This move was probably linked with the deteriorating situation in the war against the heretics and the loss of Toulouse which occurred later in that year. Faced with the possibility of expulsion from Toulouse if his patron Simon de Montfort should lose his grip, Dominic adopted the same course taken by the Franciscans in their General Chapter of 1217. In this supreme gamble seven of the companions went to Paris, Dominic and others to Rome, possibly via Bologna, while the remaining few went to Madrid. The success of the order was rapid and by Dominic's death in 1221, the Order of Preachers had been placed on a firm institutional basis with a constitution of its own. He had turned his back on the heretics and instead turned to the Church as a whole transforming a tiny band of followers into a peripatetic order. In the thirteenth century Dominicans were to become the administrators of the Inquisition and leaders of theological studies in the universities. Paris and Bologna rather than Toulouse became their headquarters and the world at large became their field for conversion. The numbers of Dominicans were never to be as great as those of the Franciscans and Dominic was altogether a far less charismatic figure than Francis. There was nevertheless much mutual borrowing and interchange between the orders. One fascinating question in the light of the similarities must be whether or not the two ever met. Both were in Rome in November 1215 and again in the early months of 1217 but there is no evidence that they met although Dominic's apparent change of heart about going into the world may give rise to the suspicion that they may indeed have done so.

Certainly 1217 saw parallel developments in the sending out of both groups of friars on long preaching tours all over their world. While preaching was fundamental to both groups an intellectual content existed to a much lesser degree among the early Franciscans. The Dominican life was based on the preparation for preaching and for them the university was of paramount importance whereas for the Franciscans it was only secondary. The prologue to the Dominican Constitutions gave brothers discretionary powers to put aside any unusual obligations if these should get in the way of studying and preaching. On the question of poverty the Dominicans were always able to own their own houses, which gave them greater stability as they expanded. On the question of manual labour and work in general it was regarded as better that a preacher should spend his time preaching or preparing to preach and that he should be supported by some source other than his own labour rather than that he should work. It is even possible that Dominic may have considered the use of lay brothers or *conversi* to care for all the preachers' needs.

The Chapter of 1220 decided that the brothers should never handle money nor receive alms in the form of cash. There was a strong concept of obedience amonst the Dominicans especially to bishops and Dominic himself set up another friar as abbot of the congregation in 1217 although retaining ultimate direction himself. There was thus little danger of him becoming the centre of controversy in the order. The Constitutions of the order with which Dominic had supplemented the Rule of St Augustine contained what was distinctive to the order especially those sections or Distinctions which described the system of provinces, officials, committees or chapters. In sharp contrast to the Franciscans the Dominicans considered that the Holy Spirit worked in the long run through the General Chapter and that their observance would be best fulfilled and safeguarded if everything they had to know and do was clearly set down.

In the early 1220s Jacques de Vitry observed the Dominicans in Bologna. He did not call them Dominicans but simply wrote about the 'new religion and preaching of the canons of Bologna'. Clearly he was describing a group of regular canons who were observing the canonical hours and living according to the Rule of St Augustine. 'Completely willing to follow the naked Christ, they take alms but only for that day. They teach and study the Holy Scriptures' he reported and indicated the rapid expansion of this order in the phrase, 'they have joined an order of preachers with an order of canons'.

However different these two orders may have been both Dominicans (the Friars Preachers) and Franciscans (the Friars Minor) were of tremendous use to the papacy in identifying the Church with the apostolic message and were indeed used by it as truly apostolic orders working in the community and having a direct line of communication with the pope himself. Previously the popes had had to use the Cistercians, who were not truly in sympathy with local communities, particularly the towns, and failed to appreciate the aspirations of lay people to be good Christians and at the same time to lead normal lives. The greatest contribution of the mendicant orders was to come later in the thirteenth century, with far-reaching implications, not only for the development of the Church but also for the growth of universities, setting up courses of study for the training of their members and providing an important part of their faculties. As the Church developed from and reacted to the extraordinary intellectual rebirth that had begun in the latter part of the twelfth century and flowered in the thirteenth, a large proportion of the most original scholars of the day was included in the membership of the friars — Albertus Magnus and Thomas Aquinas among the Dominicans, Duns Scotus and Roger Bacon among the Franciscans. A long way perhaps from Caleruega and Assisi.

5
Religious women

Women have always played a major role in the Christian religion since the time of the apostles though most have chosen the part of the active Martha rather than that of the contemplative Mary. Whilst there were anchoresses or female recluses in the Egyptian deserts, matching the hermits, there were also many groups of women living together in religious communities like their male counterparts. Jerome and Augustine both gave advice to these groups of women and suggested forms of organization to them. Augustine's famous Letter 211 contained the elements of a rule for such a community of religious women and came later to be known as the *Regula Sororum*. It is generally held that this was written *c.* 420 for the sister of Augustine and her followers and was very far from being a complete guide to the religious life. It consisted of an exhortation to lead the common life as the necessary condition for religious perfection. The Rule of St Benedict made no particular provision for women though those religious communities which existed in the early Middle Ages probably took some version of it as their model. Certainly by the seventh and eighth centuries, in France as in England, there existed many large and important nunneries which catered for noble widows and daughters. The so-called double monasteries which might, as at Whitby, have an abbess at their heads, had also communities of monks attached to them to provide the sacraments and to deal with administration. Such double monasteries, together with their commanding abbesses, had communities of monks and nuns to serve them but had, by the tenth century, ceased to exist. Any other nunneries tended to be few in number, aristocratic in patronage and exclusive in entry. By the late eleventh and early twelfth centuries it was quite clear that the circumstances of society were such that women were not going to accept exclusion from the novel forms of religious life which were than developing and which had as their main aim the practice of the *vita apostolica*.

It was obvious that there had to be a response on the part of the Church to this feminine desire for the religious life: what this response was to be was far less certain. While nunneries them-selves remained exclusive and few in number there were large numbers of women whose religious aspirations were still in need of satisfaction. That women were notoriously liable to be attracted by heretical preachers was well understood by the Church, which had witnessed the large and heterogeneous female following of wandering preachers such as Robert of Arbrissel and Norbert of Xanten. Most of the new movements and orders of the twelfth century had followers of both sexes. The majority could be divided rather arbitrarily into those orders in which women played a part from the beginning and were welcomed by the founders and those whose leaders refused to acknowledge women who claimed to be their disciples or members of their order. There was a third category, the beguines, who formed a movement for women which was substantially different from all the other groups in that it was not merely an appendix to a male movement but was a movement in its own right. The beguines may have been the heirs to one small group about which we know very little. These were the *licoisae* described by the anonymous author of the *Book of the Different Orders and Callings in the Church* (*Libellus de Diversis Ordinibus et Professionibus qui sunt in Aecclesia*) which was a guide for founders and benefactors written in the first half of the twelfth century by a regular canon in the diocese of Liège. In its prologue the author mentioned the possibility of a second book in which he was planning to discuss both male and female hermits, nuns and recluses and also *licoisae*, women living a religious life. We do not know who these *licoisae* were but we do know that the intensity of desire for a religious life was nowhere greater than in the diocese of Liège and in the areas of Brabant and Flanders known as Lotharingia. This tradition of religious women in the Liège area is further developed upon by Jacques de Vitry when describing foundations of Cistercian nuns and this Beguine movement.

Cluniacs and Benedictines

In spite of the hundreds of male houses founded over the years in association with Cluny only one house for nuns was produced, the foundation of St Hugh at Marcigny in 1055 in the diocese of Autun. Yet this marked a stage in the development of the religious

life for women. Only in the seventh century had the Benedictine
Rule been definitely adopted by nuns and even so Benedictinism
never held the same unrivalled place amongst women that it did
amongst men. Marcigny may well have been founded with St
Hugh's own mother and sister in mind and it is evident that Hugh
himself was well aware of the low esteem in which nunneries were
held. Hugh set the highest standards of discipline at Marcigny and
contemporaries wondered at the severity of the life there. It is not
known whether Hugh gave a rule to Marcigny or simply laid down
specific customs. Certainly by the early twelfth century there was
evidence to suggest that life was still strict. The Cistercians criticized Marcigny on two counts, firstly that they doubted the
wisdom and possibility of so strict a religious life for women and
secondly that it should not have been incorporated into the
Cluniac male family. These women were provided with two types
of religious life at Marcigny, the cenobitic and the eremitic. Peter
the Venerable described the life of the nuns as devoted to manual
work, psalmody and prayer which they undertook with the
strength and devotion of men. He was well acquainted with this
life since his mother held the office of cellarer and he recorded her
efforts to fulfil her charge in this respect. Of the eremitic element
all that is known is that Thurstan, Archbishop of York had invited
the recluse Christina of Markyate to go to Marcigny. Enclosure at
the convent was extremely severe and in a Bull confirming the
privileges of the convent Pope Urban II described the nuns as
enclosed and dead to the world so that they could be entirely
occupied with God. A priory of monks which was established
alongside the convent and completely separated from it provided
for the spiritual and temporal needs of the women. Numbers were
eventually limited to 99 and this complement was fully
maintained in the twelfth century. Unlike the practice for men at
Cluny, no one under the age of 21 could enter and there was to be a
'test of the spirit' to make sure the women had a strong sense of
vocation. The convent housed a cross-section from the leading
families of Europe who brought dowries with them when they
joined. Many in the community were widows or married women
who had mutually agreed with their husbands to enter the
religious life so that while they went to Marcigny their husbands
went to Cluny. Such agreements were by no means uncommon and
were certainly paralleled by lay people who also separated for
religious reasons at the time.

Another interesting insight into the Benedictine life for women is provided by Heloise (*c.* 1100–*c.*1163) who in a letter to Abelard (*c.* 1079–*c.*1156), asked, on behalf of her community, for information about the origins of the order of nuns and for advice on a rule suitable for women. In *c.* 1129 she had become the abbess of the convent of the Paraclete near Troyes and she gave a description of the way in which she had spent the previous 14 years living reluctantly under the Benedictine Rule, having been sent to the convent by Abelard. Her questions and criticisms indicated conditions similar to those severe ones at Marcigny and Heloise raised the whole question of the same burden being laid upon women as upon men, the same on the weaker sex as on the stronger. She questioned whether the one Rule of St Benedict, although professed in the Church by women and men equally, was not clearly meant to be fully obeyed only by men since it was written for them alone. Why should women be concerned with what the Rule said about cowls and scapulars? How could they be concerned with the instruction that woollen garments should be worn next to the skin? And what about the obligation to hospitality? Should an abbess disobey the Rule by not offering hospitality or should she eat with the men she had allowed to enter the convent? Should nuns go out to labour in the fields or, as Gregory the Great had advised in *Pastoral Care*, should they be treated differently from men 'for heavy burdens may be laid upon men but lighter burdens on women who should be gently converted by less exacting means'. As Heloise said, with more than a flash of humour, 'this showed plainly enough that the neck of the bullock and heifer should in no sense be brought under the same yoke of a common Rule since those whom nature created unequal could not properly be made equal in labour'. In support of her claim that the Rule was only for men she referred with considerable insight to Benedict's moderation. This she considered would have been even greater had he wished to provide for the weaker sex whose frailty and infirmity were generally known.

Fontevrault, Prémontré and the Gilbertines

Several of the wandering preachers, in particular Robert of Arbrissel and Norbert of Xanten, attracted large crowds of women to them and these had to be settled into convents to avoid scandal. Robert of Arbrissel settled his female followers at Fontevrault in the Loire Valley in 1100 in a community that was heterogeneous because he was reluctant to send anyone away. The various buildings at Fontevrault demonstrate Robert's desire to provide for all who followed him. A building dedicated to the Virgin Mary housed the virgins, widows and matrons; penitents including former prostitutes were placed under the guidance of Mary Magdalene; the sick lived in a house dedicated to St Lazarus. Men were placed in a house dedicated to St John the Evangelist who, as Christ had wished, attached himself to the Virgin after his death. Although the social composition of the house was at first varied, so great was its success, that within a generation, it became exclusively aristocratic.

Norbert of Xanten, founder of the Premontratensian canons, attracted large crowds of women in northern France and the Low Countries and settled them in the revived institution of the double monastery at Prémontré in 1121. The women were subject to a very severe discipline and were instructed to care for the poor and the sick. Such houses were popular and there was a flood of recruits. In 1137 the General Chapter decreed the separation of nuns and monks, possibly only for reasons of convenience, although successive popes repeated that adequate maintenance should be provided for women. By 1150, apparently undeterred by the powerful forces at work against them, the women were said to number over 10,000. Finally in 1198 Innocent III's bull *De non recipiendis sororibus* confirmed and commended the decision of the General Chapter no longer to accept them into the order.

An English attempt, local but most interesting, to create a community for women served by lay brothers and lay sisters occurred in the first half of the twelfth century. In or about 1131, Gilbert of Sempringham, a Lincolnshire priest, had enclosed seven local girls and at their request had provided a rule of life for them. Some women employed to serve the nuns were incorporated into the community and very soon lay brothers were introduced on the Cistercian model. The Gilbertines followed closely Cistercian practices yet were in no way formally affiliated to the Cistercian Order. The experiment attracted a great deal of interest and support from all levels of society for provision was made for village girls as well as for aristocratic women. In 1147, with his nuns already following a modified version of the Cistercian example, Gilbert went to Cîteaux to get approval from the General Chapter for the affiliation of his houses to the Cistercian Order. Instead

Eugenius III instituted Gilbert the head of his community and Gilbert and St Bernard together drew up the Gilbertine Rule between 1147 and 1148. The refusal of the Cistercians to take on the Gilbertines may possibly be explained by their additional obligations undertaken at the Chapter of 1147 for the houses of the Orders of Savigny and Obazine.

The Gilbertine Constitutions borrowed widely for the rules it used to govern each of the four divisions of the Order. The nuns followed a modified Benedictine rule which stressed complete seclusion and a total absence of all chanting and music. The canons who served the nuns were to follow the Rule of St Augustine while lay brothers or *conversi* were organized along Cistercian lines. Gilbert is known to have modified this section of his Rule dealing with the *conversi* but this appears not to have prevented a revolt amongst them in the late 1160s. The most original part of this Rule was that concerning the lay sisters where existing practices were codified. The centralized organization of the Gilbertines, with its Annual General Chapter and strict limitations on new foundations, was clearly modelled on Cistercian lines, often going further than the Cistercians. An innovation by the Gilbertines was the introduction of a supreme head or Master of the Order to provide essential control and to avoid scandal. The Gilbertine Constitutions derived from the Rule of St Benedict, from the Premonstratensians, the Augustinians and the Order of Fontevrault as well as from the Cistercians. All these orders had adaptations to suit the peculiar condition of communities of strictly enclosed nuns served by chaplains and lay brothers. Certainly without the impulse of St Bernard and Pope Eugenius III it is unlikely that the Gilbertine communities would have survived. By the end of the 1180s there were some 700 canons and 1,500 nuns and the Gilbertines had become the fastest growing order in England. This represented a unique expression of English monasticism which, while it drew heavily on other rules, might never have succeeded at all had it not been for the rejection by the Cistercians on the one hand and help from St Bernard on the other.

Cistercian nuns

By the end of the twelfth century a phenomenon had occurred in parts of Europe which would have seemed impossible to the early Cistercians. Large numbers of women began to live together in communities calling themselves Cistercians. They claimed that their convents followed the customs of Cîteaux yet their existence was consistently denied by the male branch of the order, which displayed a marked hostility to women. Not until 1213 did a decree of the Cistercian General Chapter specifically deal with convents of women and thus reverse the contention that a Cistercian nun was a contradiction in terms.

The very strictness of the order may have attracted the women although, from what we know of most other foundations, all seemed to have been very firmly controlled. We know that several women lived within the shelter of Molesme and it is quite likely that the nearby priory of Jully may have been founded to accommodate the wives and dependants of the new recruits to Cîteaux. St Bernard's sister and sister-in-law both entered this priory. The foundation of a further convent at Tart reflected the foundation of Cîteaux itself as a breakaway group. Some nuns from Jully, dissatisfied with life there, asked the third abbot of Cîteaux, Stephen Harding, to help them follow a stricter vocation. In spite of their apparent close proximity to and relationship with Cîteaux neither Jully nor Tart ever claimed in the twelfth century that they were Cistercian. There were many however who did, claiming to imitate the customs of Cîteaux and the fervour of the return to a stricter observance of the primitive Benedictine Rule. The Cistercians' rejection of women was based on their contention that women were too fragile to live up to such a harsh life, *aspera vita*. Jacques de Vitry agreed that the view that women were too frail to aspire to the severity and perfection of the order's way of life might have been justified at its inception. In his day he was not so sure. He had seen a huge flood of devoted virgins and holy women assuming the regular habit in such numbers that he compared them to stars in the sky and in the diocese of Liège alone he had seen the foundation and construction of seven Cistercian nunneries with three times more applicants than there were places for them. He linked this expansion with the refusal of the Premonstratensians to admit any more women. He was able to say this because Walter, abbot of Villers (1214–1221) in the diocese of Liège, was an active patron of Cistercian nunneries for he 'desired nothing more in this world than to lead men into the religious life and to found convents for young girls'.

While, generally speaking, there was in the twelfth century very little evidence to show that these nunneries were Cistercian, by the turn of the century some houses of women claimed to be so. The famous Spanish convent of Las Huelgas founded in 1187 seems to have been the first to have claimed to be Cistercian although, in this case, the powerful patron was Alfonso VIII of Castile to whom even the abbot of Cîteaux may well have deferred. Official recognition of nuns and their organization within the Cistercian Order was eventually conceded by the statute of 1213 whereby the General Chapter reluctantly acknowledged their existence and was forced to attempt to discipline them. The number of nuns was restricted; they were to be strictly enclosed; they were forbidden to receive visitors and their opportunities for confession were strictly limited. The earlier reluctance of the Cistercians to accept nuns within the order was, at least in part, linked with the troubles they had encountered in trying to discipline them and it was hoped that the Statute of 1213 would remedy this situation. By 1228, the General Chapter took a further step and issued a pre-emptory statute forbidding all further attachment of nunneries to the order and refusing the benefit of visitation and pastoral care to existing communities. Despite this, the numbers of women claiming to be Cistercian continued to increase and between 1220 and 1240 almost 50 houses for women were incorporated into the order in places as far apart as Castile and Hungary, Ghent and Marseille.

Beguines

Those religious women known as beguines were located mainly in the Low Countries. They formed what was basically a women's movement which differed from all earlier movements in the Church in being distinctly feminine and not merely an appendage to those movements which owed their impetus, direction and support to the activities of men. Contemporary male observers were, on the whole, favourable to the beguines. Caesarius of Heisterbach (c. 1180–c. 1240) reported that the religious women of Liège, whilst they lived in the world in secular dress together with secular people, often surpassed in charity those who were cloistered. 'In the midst of worldly people they were spiritual, in the midst of pleasure seekers they were pure and in the midst of noise and confusion they led a serene, eremitic life'. The beguines were a lay religious group which developed within the confines of the principalities of Brabant-Flanders, an area which members of this group called Lotharingia, and later spread to northern France and the Rhineland. Their movement was essentially urban with no definite rule to live by and no real founder. They had no authority from the hierarchy and imposed no irreversible vows upon their followers. They aimed to live according to the *vita apostolica*, leading lives of chastity if young girls or continence if widows, all renouncing worldly goods. They did not protest at the wealth of others but voluntarily renounced property and possessions to fulfil their evangelical ideal. They lived by manual labour and made no burdensome demands on their fellow men. Grosseteste, bishop of Lincoln, in *c.* 1230 said that this was a most perfect and most holy form of the religious life, living as they did by the work of their own hands.

Several contemporary religious observers selected this movement as being something new, different and special in the religous life of the period. The first observer to note the existence of the beguines and indeed to be closely involved with them, was Jacques de Vitry who wrote a *Life* of Mary of Oignies (*c.* 1177–1213) the 'new saint' of the diocese of Liège. Irresistibly attracted to the practice of voluntary personal poverty from her youth, she had renounced her marriage, distributed her wealth to the poor and, together with her husband, had gone to serve a leper colony near Nivelles. After several years, during which this life devoted to poverty had brought her more fame than she would have wished, she moved to a cell at the Augustinian priory of St Nicholas at Oignies where she lived in complete poverty save for what she earned at her spindle. Jacques de Vitry was drawn to Oignies by her fame and by his desire to identify himself with her work. At her instigation he was ordained in 1210 and remained in the community as her confessor. We know that he referred to her as his 'spiritual mother', *mater spiritualis* and that she helped him a great deal in the preparation of his sermons. After her death in 1213 he continued to be the enthusiastic protector of her followers and, in her memory, carried with him everywhere her finger in a reliquary. At the instigation of Bishop Fulk of Toulouse, who must have had in mind the community at Prouille in his own diocese, Jacques de Vitry wrote her *Life*, not only to enhance her memory but expressly to counter heresy in the south of France by describing the extraordinary piety and devotion of the holy women of Lotharingia who had resisted heresy.

The beguine movement, however much it might be accused of heresy, was not an heretical movement. The beguines made no

controversial demands on the clergy and did not stress to the same
extent as heretics the need for personal merit in the priesthood.
Beguines were often confused with heretics particularly as it was
from their supposed Albigensian affiliations that their name
derived. Jacques de Vitry discounted the accusations of hetero-
doxy against them and in his role as protector worked to save them
from this charge. The beguines fascinated him by the fervour and
spontaneity of their personal religion and he saw that if they could
be contained within the Church in common with the Humiliati and
the Poor Catholics they could provide a further effective barrier
against heresy.

Jacques de Vitry was interested in pious women's communities
because he saw them as being significant and potentially useful to
the Church. His enthusiasm for the beguines led him to wish for
their complete incorporation into the ecclesiastical structure so
that their obedience might be assured and he became an active propagandist on their behalf. In 1216 John de Liro, his friend and
preacher in the Liège area, had set out for Rome to see the pope and
to make representations on behalf of the beguines but was lost
in the Alps. In the spring of the same year Jacques de Vitry had
himself started out to see Innocent III at Perugia where the curia
then was but his arrival coincided with the death of that pope and
he saw instead Honorius III, from whom he only managed to
obtain an oral permission for the beguines in Flanders, France and
the empire to live together in religious communities and to assist
one another in mutual exhortation. This was the most that could
have been expected following the decree of the Lateran Council
and the death of Innocent III.

At the turn of the twelfth century the beguines lived as
'religiously' as they could according to strict evangelical precepts,
individually or in small groups, either with their parents or in their
own houses. After the oral permission for their association in 1216
they grouped themselves into semi-organized groups under a
mistress and often followed the practices of a convent. The
beguines tended to become more enclosed, finally separated from
the world and moved to a beguinage, a complex of buildings which,
as at Bruges or Ghent, might have several hundred women living
under a rule with their own chapel and cemetery and with a priest
to have cure of souls, celebrate the office, administer the sacraments, hear their confessions and bury their dead.

Although the Fourth Lateran Council of 1215 had forbidden the creation of new orders the beguines of the Low Countries, by their numbers and by their religiosity, had forced the Church into a devious form of action. They were increasingly controlled by being institutionalized in much the same way as those women who at that time were attaching themselves to the mendicant orders. This institutionalization, which was an effective method of silencing their detractors, helped the Church to weaken the originality of the beguine vocation by implicitly assimilating them into the category of religious orders.

The special religious importance of the beguines of the Low Countries was emphasized by the contemporary canonist Henry de Susa when he said, 'In a broad sense one calls religious those who lived in a saintly fashion and religiously in their own houses, not because they submit themselves to a precise rule but because of their life style which is harder and more simple than that of other lay people who live in a purely worldly fashion'.

St Clare and the order of St Damian

The recognition of Francis and his followers had very wide implications for Clare (c. 1193–1253) who was received into the religious life at the age of 18 in 1212. The oral permission given to Francis in 1210 contained no justification for the formation of a female order nor was such permission subsequently issued. After her conversion by Francis Clare established her community in the church of St Damian in Assisi which Francis had rebuilt. The community did not follow any usual recognized rule but a simple *formula vitae* based on a life of evangelical poverty which was essentially similar to his own and a profession of obedience to him. When in 1215 the Lateran Council imposed on all new movements the obligation to accept an approved rule the community at St Damian had to apply for a special privilege to enable it to maintain its renunciation of property and its profession of strict poverty. There was clearly a price to be paid for this. The contemporary evidence of Jacques de Vitry described the Franciscans and the Poor Clares working closely together and was entirely consistent with the indications that Francis originally intended women to play as central a part in his activities as men and that their roles at first were not so different as they later became. He certainly indicated that the enclosure of the sisters was not very strict while living and working in hospices and it is likely that Clare may not have wanted strict claustration at all. The price to be paid for recognition was henceforth that Clare should be abbess of St Damian and that the community should be strictly claustrated. She received from Innocent III the *privilegium paupertatis* or privilege of poverty which allowed the sisters of St Damian to live without an assured income. All previously approved rules had been based on the presupposition that each community required a sufficient income from corporate possessions to maintain itself although individuals remained without property. This privilege represented for Clare a guarantee that her community would not be obliged to adopt an existing rule and its uniqueness was clearly recognized by Innocent III who wrote it joyfully with his own hand (*cum hilaritate magna*). It seemed that Innocent had therefore helped her to create an entirely new form of convent community which maintained itself on alms and the profits of manual labour in the same way as the Franciscans. The privilege may have been issued in 1215 when Clare was made abbess or as late as May 1216 when Innocent was in Perugia but at whatever time, whether before, during or after the Lateran Council, it was unquestionably in opposition to the Council's decree since it made possible a new form of female religious community not based on any existing religious order.

In spite of this, in later life Francis did everything he could to prevent the sort of cooperation which he seemed to have envisaged earlier even rejecting the use of the word 'sister' and warning his brothers against the snares of female companionship. It was essential for the Franciscan order to avoid any suspicion of familiarity with women so that it could establish its respectability before the hierarchy at large in the 1220s. St Damian's was given a rule in 1219 by Cardinal Hugolino which was intended to cover a whole group of houses for there was certainly a tremendous demand from women all over Italy to join similar religious groups. The exact text of this first rule was lost and a substantially revised version was reissued in 1239 when Hugolino had become Pope Gregory IX. It was basically Benedictine with considerable stress on enclosure, communal property, essential for an enclosed life, a short novitiate and much apparent Cistercian influence. Clare resisted all threats to her special privilege and any suggestion that she was not bound to the rule of St Francis and to poverty. It was not until 1253 that Innocent IV confirmed her own version of the *privilegium paupertatis* and also that essential characteristic of her rule, the profession of the strict principle of apostolic poverty in accordance with the directions of Francis, which represented a personal privilege for Clare and her community of St Damian.

Cathar women

Among the Cathars women could become ministers or *perfectae*, which they could not do within the Catholic Church. The Cathar sacrament of the *consolamentum* was only administered to those who had successfully completed a long and rigorous period of training and had vowed to lead lives of chastity, purity and absolute poverty. The lives of these *perfectae* were henceforth devoted to preaching, conversion and contemplation, travelling around the countryside in pairs with another *perfecta*. It seemed that there was no distinction between male and female in the Cathar ministry which, if really so, must have presented a positive advantage over the Christian faith to women. Women could be brought up to be *perfectae* in the same way as child oblates within the Christian Church. These children were trained in the equivalent of a convent, or even in a family group, for the importance of the early environment in transmitting Catharism could be very great. Whilst it was possible to be a very young recruit to Catharism other women could receive the *consolamentum* at a more mature age in the same way as one might enter a convent in later life in the Church. A Cathar women could provide the same spiritual services as a man and was entitled to the same respect and support as a male *perfectus*.

The importance of women amongst the ministers of Cathars was matched by their role amongst the believers or *credentes*. Believers provided accommodation, resting places at which preachers could stay and houses where food and safe shelter were provided. The role of women in Catharism was thus important whether as *perfectae* or as believers. It seems that participation was widespread and that up to one third of Cathars may have been women. Dominic's foundation at Prouille in 1206 demonstrated his recognition of the nature and spread of Catharism and the dangers of schools being used in the recruiting of Cathar girls. In cases of warfare, impoverishment or numerous co-heirs, the daughters of the nobility would be cared for in Cathar houses. Although women were admitted to the Cathar ministry there are no known examples of women amongst the bishops or deacons.

The significance of the role of women in Languedoc is difficult to explain. The local society might provide some possible explanations. Primogeniture was not so widespread as elsewhere and women could inherit responsible positions as landholders, a responsibility which could help them to be recognized and accepted in other fields. The Cathar ministry wanted no landed endowments for itself although willing to accept gifts of money and of houses for the *perfecti* and this may well have created sympathy for them amongst the local nobles. Everyone tolerated heresy, everyone had friends who were heretics and many heretics often lived quite openly. In this more open society diverse views and attitudes would have been more acceptable including those towards women. A social structure which allowed for strong female influence also offered examples of strong-minded women prepared to defy their families. The powers of patronage which women might possess and the role of the matriarchal figure were also of importance. It is possible that there were houses, very like beguinages, where women could live together in voluntary poverty and chastity. The orthodox equivalent of such houses were called *reclusaniae* in Toulouse. Cathars were keenly interested in the *vita apostolica* and were seen to be leading the lives of the apostles. It must surely be highly significant that Fulk of Toulouse commissioned the *Life* of Mary of Oignies from Jacques de Vitry so that he could take it back to his heretical diocese as an example of one group at least of holy women within the Church who were a match for their heretical sisters in Languedoc. Seen in this context this *Life* must be one of the most significant works of the early thirteenth century. It was written with a real and urgent purpose in mind and enables us to understand more fully the way in which religious women responded to the spiritual reawakening of the twelfth and early thirteenth centuries.

6
Reaction of Church and papacy

During this period of great spiritual reawakening and theological ferment the Church, under the leadership of the papacy, had aimed to maintain its authority, look to its organization and defeat any outright heresy which might appear. It could not, nor could its hierarchy, be unaware of or unconcerned with the religious fervour associated with the *vita apostolica*; the return to the basic principles of the Christian religion of New Testament times and the identification with the historical appearance on earth of Jesus Christ its founder. The Papacy, having already achieved its own reform in the eleventh century under the leadership of reformers such as Gregory VII and others and under the influence of Cluny, felt that there was no need for further reforms. Its aim was to proceed towards achieving a period of stable development and it was not eager to embark on a continuation of reform. However the questions raised in the ferment of the times and the types of organization put forward to realize widespread religious aspirations could not be ignored. Direct confrontation was avoided. The Cistercians and the other new orders which followed them were recognized and even encouraged, including that of St Francis, in spite of growing apprehension about the proliferation of such orders. Moreover the Church succeeded in turning them to its own service and whilst this may have been to its benefit it was perhaps not really satisfactory in keeping intact the aims and objectives of those who founded and developed the new orders. Indeed it was one further element to add to those occurring internally which led to the decay and consequent need for yet more reform of these orders which had once seemed to carry all before them. Individual popes, including such outstanding ones as Urban II (1188—1099), Alexander III (1159—1181) and Innocent III (1198—1216) acting with their curias or, on certain occasions, with councils of the whole Church held at the Lateran Palace in Rome, were called upon to react, to compromise and to give way more than a little, in order to maintain a united Church in the face of the continuing problems

of the period which just would not go away. At certain times
however the Church needed to restate the force of its authority and
the results of these activities can plainly be seen in the decisions of
the Third Lateran Council of 1179, the decree *ad abolendam* of
1184 and the decisions of the Fourth Lateran Council of 1215.

The Third Lateran Council 1179

The great Lateran Councils of the Church in the twelfth century,
1123, 1139 and 1179 had at least one thing in common. They were
all held soon after a papal schism or some other sort of trouble
which affected the papacy. Various views were put forward both
prior to and during these Councils before any decisions were
arrived at. Many were against increasing the number of conciliar
decrees as they would cause great confusion and multiply the
number of transgressors against these laws. To illustrate this
point, Peter the Chanter cited the plea of a certain Master Ivo of
Chartres delivered before the Third Lateran Council of 1179. Ivo
had warned the conciliar fathers neither to renew the old decretals
nor to establish new ones lest the Council be 'convoked in vain'. He
considered that such decretals, by providing the opportunity for
disobedience, only encouraged wrangling amongst scholars and
lawyers. Even when they were useful these new inventions should
be set aside lest their numbers became overwhelming. He wanted
the Council to command observance of the Holy Gospel which as
he reported, many honoured only in the breach. On the other hand,
in the inaugural session of Lateran III, Rufinus, bishop of Assisi,
envisaged as the purpose of the assembled council the recovery of
the Book of Law which had been lost to the multitudes. Twenty-
seven statutes were proposed. They were both comprehensive and
coordinated and were inspired by Alexander III who was himself
a canonist. In the event, at the Council itself, 12 statutes were
actually rejected and contemporaries regarded this as quite
unprecedented.

The Council was set against the background of the anti-heretical
campaign in the Toulouse area led by Henry of Marcy, abbot of
Clairvaux and which was in need of support. Canon XXVII condemned Cathars, Patarines, Publicans and diverse heretics and
deprived them of their goods and possessions without stating the
precise doctrines they were supposed to have held. This had
dangers for both the Waldensians and the Humiliati who formed

simple Gospel-based movements whose members desired the right
to exhort and to care for their fellow Christians. As this might
entail preaching and the cure of souls these groups too were in
danger of being pushed from disobedience into heresy. Both the
anonymous Chronicler of Laon and the English satirist Walter
Map reported that Valdes attended the Council with a group of
followers, showed their vernacular translations and asked for
papal approval and authorization for their preaching. The details
given by Map of his discussions with the Waldensians may be
superficial but it was clear that there was certainly some theological examination of them personally when they presented themselves to the pope. The Laon Chronicler tells us that Alexander III
embraced Valdes, approved his vow of voluntary poverty but
would not allow him to preach unless invited to do so by the local
clergy. This really amounted to a prohibition since these clergy
were most unlikely to issue such an invitation. This concern of
Lateran III with heresy supports the view that heresy as such only
appeared after 1100 and that its rise must be reckoned as one of the
most dramatic aspects of the twelfth century. The western Church
was faced for the first time with the problem of mass apostasy.
This fact must have been uppermost in the minds of Church
leaders when forming the decree *ad abolendam* a few years later.

Ad abolendam 1184

In 1184 the papal decree *ad abolendam* excommunicated several
groups who were considered by the Church to be dangerously
active in their protest concerning the purity of the Church's
precepts. In thus seeking to bring about discipline and unity,
Lucius III (1181–1185) ensured that the immediate future of these
groups would be one of official conflict with orthodoxy even
though it was clearly not the wish of most of these groups that this
should be so. Covered by this decree were not only the dualist
Cathars but also groups of Humiliati and Waldensians who wished
only to lead lives according to the *vita apostolica* communicating
their experience of this Christian way of life to others.

The decree *ad abolendam* may be seen as the first real attempt to
define an official attitude to manifest dissent. Whole groups of
heretics, listed as Cathars, Patarines, Humiliati or those falsely
called Poor of Lyon, Passagians, Josephines and Arnaldists, were

indiscriminately anathematized. Two distinct groups of deviants were mentioned: the first were those who had claimed for themselves the right to preach publicly or privately without papal authorization and the second were those who taught doctrines contrary to the Church on sacramental questions. As a result of the decree Valdes and his followers were not strictly speaking heretics but anathematized schismatics. Judgement was made not on their doctrines but on their tenacious contumacy. They had lapsed into disobedience because they would not observe the proscription of preaching. They and other groups akin to them remained impenitent, certain of their apostolic vocation and their right to represent the true Christian Church.

Other provisions of the decree declared that clerics were to be degraded and handed over to the secular power if they themselves were found to subscribe to heretical beliefs or even to know that certain people were heretics. Bishops who failed to publish these penalties were to be suspended for three years. Any three respectable people in each diocese could denounce, on oath to their bishop, those who held secret conventicles or who differed in their way of life from the faithful. For the first time regular inquisitions were to be held and the guilty punished by the secular power according to their transgressions.

The *Distinctio* of Innocent III

When in 1198 Innocent III became pope the effects of the decree *ad abolendam* soon came to his attention. Such an arbitrary and all-embracing excommunication was not in line with his aim of increasing Church unity. As he saw it, groups who were simply misguided would only increase the true unity of the Church if they were allowed to work within its framework rather than being officially excluded. Innocent's methods of leading the groups back into the Church bore witness to his breadth of vision and his ability to put into perspective the problem of the rapidly growing number of dissident groups. Innocent III was eminently approachable. He encouraged all those who wished to come to him at the Curia to do so. He understood both their weaknesses and their strengths and used their inherent wish to remain in conformity with the Church as a basis for his actions. In doing so he was able to get them to agree to take urgent and necessary oaths although they had a revulsion to oath-taking which they justified by reference to James 5:12, and to agree to the shedding of blood when those in authority could not otherwise avoid it, something to which they had been radically opposed. They also accepted the need for strong family groups even though they were inclined to regard marriages as earthly ties which should be loosened. His method was to get them to put forward declarations of their claims to orthodoxy in the form of *proposita*. These *proposita* were short statements indicating the willingness of these groups to devote themselves to lives of Christian piety. In dealing with these *proposita* Innocent III showed that he was prepared to encounter these protest movements as no other pope had done before. He sought to bridge the gap between the groups and the hierarchical Church as long as it could be considered that orthodox belief remained untouched and that hierarchical authority was basically recognized. He set up commissions usually of three men drawn from the regular orders and seculars to investigate this evidence. While the enquiries were proceeding the bishops were warned to cease penalties against these groups and to give protection to their goods and property. Permission to preach was granted on definite terms and under episcopal licence and, whenever appropriate, a group was placed under some sort of rule. Innocent regarded previous episcopal policies as too severe. He urged his bishops to act like doctors. Mere diagnosis of the symptoms was insufficient. Effective treatment of each case was necessary, whether by amputation of a malignant limb to save the body or by the soothing of wounds with oil not wine. Like Alexander III, his predecessor, Innocent urged that the guilty should be acquitted rather than that the innocent should be condemned and he warned his bishops that they could turn piety into heresy by harsh and precipitate action. A way back into the Church was to be opened for those unwillingly or unjustly excluded.

Innocent's achievement was to create a host of communities and groups in which the movement towards voluntary poverty was legitimized. This was especially so in regard to those mendicant preachers who were the forerunners of the friars. The policy did not represent a change in the general attitude of the religious leadership of the Church but came personally from Innocent's clear insight into the Church's task in the face of the proliferation of protesting movements. He not only established the distinction or *distinctio* between irrevocable heretics and those who were merely disobedient but also pointed out the supreme folly of excluding from the Church the latter as well as the former. Innocent was able to incorporate these disobedient groups into the hierarchical Church with great foresight, skill and energy. His policy revealed a sensitive approach to those whom he on no account wanted excluded from the Church as heretics. He recognized that because of their austere lifestyle they were able to speak to heretics on equal terms and so was willing to allow them to preach so long as they conceded that this right was linked with the special permission which he had given them. The Humiliati Tertiaries were thus able to witness to the faith and to preach on their experience of Christian life but were not allowed to teach doctrine. The followers of Durand de Huesca and Bernard Prim presented Innocent with a more difficult problem because of their peripatetic life style. When their leaders went personally to the pope — and it should be stressed that those who went in person usually did not come away empty-handed — they were subjected to a test of belief including the required oath to authority. Once they had conceded that the right to preach was linked with a papal commission they received approval to preach as a community. The requests of Francis were met on rather different terms. As clerics he and his followers could be given the licence to preach anywhere (*licentia praedicandi ubique*), and the question of leadership became regulated when Francis promised obedience to the pope and in turn his companions promised to obey him. Innocent III was not without opponents in carrying out these conciliatory and in some ways lenient practices and it was at the Lateran Council of 1215 that a great debate was to be carried out before the necessary decisions on behalf of the whole Church were to be made.

Innocent must have worked unceasingly behind the scenes of this Fourth Lateran Council to be able to counter as far as he could the strong conservative opposition of many of the leading bishops and abbots, a large number of whom came from those orders which had themselves been new at the beginning of the twelfth century. He was able to carry out his task with such a fair measure of success because, in addition to his political, organizational and diplomatic skills, he himself understood and accepted the principles underlying the search for the *vita apostolica* which was the basis of that great spiritual reawakening and personal rebirth which came to so many during this period. To aid him in this task he was willing both to use the Church's system of canonization and also to advance the cause of crusading against pagans and perfidious heretics, which developed so strongly during this period and which he fully supported.

Innocent III and the *vita apostolica*

Of all the popes during this period, it was Innocent III who combined most successfully the personal ideals of the *vita apostolica* with the understanding of the Church's need to reform itself to meet the new situation. A vivid account of his witness to this was given by a contemporary anonymous biographer, the author of his *Gesta* who ennumerated many of the charitable acts which Innocent III performed in the year 1207 to 1208. These he used to demonstrate that dimension of the *vita apostolica* where stress was placed on the love of one's neighbours and on the corporal works of mercy.

In 1207, Innocent gave up wearing rich vestments. Instead he put on a simple tunic of undyed white wool, as an example of his piety and personal renunciation and as a possible mark of respect for the similar actions of Diego and Dominic in Languedoc. He further demonstrated this piety by providing a physical setting for his works of charity, hospitality and the care of the sick. To do this he created one of the most interesting religious corporations of the early thirteenth century by combining his new hospital foundation of Santo Spirito with the old church of the Saxon School, Santa Maria in Sassia in the Borgo area of Rome. Earlier, in 1198, Innocent, in praising the existing foundation of the Hospital of Saint-Esprit in Montpellier under the leadership of Guy, declared it to be a shining example of a place where corporal works of mercy — feeding the hungry, giving drink to the thirsty, welcoming strangers, clothing the poor and tending and burying the sick — were being carried out. At some time between 1198 and 1204, Guy of Montpellier himself must have come to Rome for, on 19 June 1204, a Bull placed him at the head of the new hospital foundation of Santo Spirito on the banks of the Tiber. Innocent paid for the erection of this hospital with the declared aim of reproducing in Rome the ideal of charity as practised by Christ. The first task for the hospital had been to deal with the problem of abandoned children whose corpses were so frequently fished from the Tiber. A box placed next to the door of the hospital allowed people to deposit their unwanted babies at any hour of the day or night. It was clearly understood that no awkward questions would be asked, no furtive glances taken and no names sought out. This hospital also catered for women in labour, even providing a series of cradles so that each baby might sleep alone and thus avoid the danger of being over-laid by its mother. The children were later raised by the Sisters of the Hospital. Young boys were apprenticed to a suitable trade whilst the girls were provided with marriage dowries unless they proved to have a vocation. Female sinners, many of whom were prostitutes, were admitted during Holy and Easter Weeks if they were truly penitent. The Hospital was not designed solely for mothers and their babies. Once a week, the Brothers of the Hospital were instructed to go out into the streets and actually seek out both male and female infirm paupers so that they might be brought back for nursing and care. The Rule observed here was Augustinian and Guy, as Rector, was placed in charge of the two hospitals, in Montpellier as well as in Rome. This arrangement, although understandable, was not ideal since the two houses were many miles apart, separated one from the other by the Alps.

In 1208, Innocent instituted a yearly liturgical station at the Hospital of Santo Spirito. At this solemn procession was carried the Veronica, the relic of the towel which bore the imprint of Christ's face at his Crucifixion and which signified his suffering for others. This procession, from the Basilica of St Peter's where the Veronica was kept, took place on the first Sunday after Epiphany, the day on which the Church recited in its Gospel liturgy the marriage feast at Cana. Innocent seemed to have believed that he would find in the Hospital the six vats of water of which the Gospels spoke transformed into wine. These vats were placed in the Hospital to represent the corporal works of mercy. They were, metaphorically, always to be found full in this pious house since works of charity were accomplished there in all their fullness. The ceremony was carried out with great pomp with Innocent himself, surrounded by his cardinals, following the procession. He celebrated mass and preached a homily based on the Gospel for the day so that the people, as he said, should not leave hungry from these mystical wedding celebrations. Nor did he forget the poor at this feast. One thousand paupers from the surrounding area, together with the 300 inmates of the Hospital, would each receive

three pence taken from the papal treasury, one for bread, one for
meat and the third for wine. Innocent hoped and indeed expected
that his example would be followed elsewhere by churchmen in
witness to the meaning of the apostolic life.

Innocent III's use of canonization — the case of Homobono

The right of the papacy to canonization allowed it control over the
nature and contents of the devotions for which it demanded
approval. To meet the great flood of candidates being put forward
for sainthood in the twelfth century new procedures had to be
devised and implemented. Sanctity was essentially, if not exclusively, defined as a collection of supernatural powers of which the
principal was that of healing the sick. Papal control over the
canonization process was traditionally exercised through a series
of inquiries which were empowered to search out the three particular signs of sanctity, healing miracles, prophesy and death 'in
the odour of sanctity'. The request for canonization had to be
supported by a *Vita* or biography of the saint. The special role
played by Innocent III was to give to this inquiry a more precise
juridical form by removing from it elements of superstition and by
stressing instead true spirituality.

The first canonization process carried out by Innocent III was
that of St Homobono of Cremona. The special interest of this case
is that, for the first time in the life of a saint, the pope placed
Homobono's life and pious works on the same footing as his
miracles. Innocent however, while maintaining the existing base
for the canonization process, affirmed in the Bull of Canonization
that neither 'merits without miracles' nor 'miracles without
merits' were in themselves sufficient as proofs of sanctity and that
any supernatural phenomenon on its own would appear
ambiguous because diabolical forces were always liable to be
present. Innocent III brought to the Church the realization that
only a man or woman with strong public support could be
designated a saint and that such support would henceforth have to
be subjected to a rigorous examination in the form of a judicial
procedure carried out by the Church.

Innocent III occupied himself above all in improving the standards of the inquiry. This new orientation can be seen in the
process of canonization of St Homobono in 1199 where the pope
personally interrogated at the Curia a special delegation of many
wise and religious men from the diocese of Cremona led by their

bishop, Sicard (1185–1215), promoter of the cause and biographer of the saint. Homobono was a married layman, a merchant whose life had been a model of religious devotion. He had attended daily mass, praying constantly, prostrating himself and repeating the divine office like a monk. His house had become a centre of charitable works from which he cared for orphans, fed the poor and arranged funerals. He had died quite suddenly in the middle of early morning mass on 13 November 1197 and his pious reputation soon led to the attribution of various miracles. The principal witness was the priest Osbert who had been his confessor for 20 years and Homobono's miracles were corroborated by a collective oath from all those present.

Not only is Homobono's canonization interesting from the procedural point of view and the move away from the purely supernatural but other reasons lay behind this action. Cremona, a centre of imperial (Ghibelline) influence, was also a centre of heresy. Homobono, himself a supporter of the Guelfs or papal faction, had worked strenuously as a peace-maker between the two groups and as a witness to the true faith. Bishop Sicard's success in obtaining the canonization of Homobono represented the earliest stage of a movement to foster lay sanctity and encourage it wherever it was to be found. It allowed Innocent III to give a more coherent formulation and wider diffusion to the juridical principles underlying the canonization inquiry. He placed a wholly new emphasis on the importance of virtue in the estimation of sanctity in line with his view of the way the *vita apostolica* should be carried out in the Church.

Innocent III and the crusade to Livonia

The crusading impulse of western Christendom, so much an established feature of the late eleventh and twelfth centuries, did not come from the frontier point of contact between Christian and Moslem. The policy of those who lived in these sensitive border lands was rather to live and let live. Instead, the zeal and pressure accompanying the crusades came from within, from the Christian power-centres of Rome and northern France and boosted by the prophetic souls of the *vita apostolica*. In the simplest terms crusades were holy wars authorized by popes and fought in the interests of the whole of Christendom. The crusaders who fought in them were placed under special vows of fidelity which freed

them from secular obligations, placing them instead under ecclesiastical protection and offering them, through indulgences,
remission of sins for their souls. Participation and deeds
performed in the crusading cause were considered to be specially
meritorious.

Crusades, so wholeheartedly accepted in the twelfth century,
were seen as essential to the mission of the Church. The success of
a crusade not only demonstrated the reinvigoration of Christendom but was also regarded as proving that mission and crusade
could only succeed against a background of Christian renewal. The
urge to preach amongst those who had responded to the *vita
apostolica* implied equally a desire to convert — not only the
infidel but also pagans in the borderlands of Christendom. A
motto for such a mission might have been 'compel them to come
in', using the reconciliation made by St Augustine of the use of
force with the power of Christian love. As in the parable of the host
at the feast who sent out his servant to compel those in the high-
ways to come in, compulsion of non-believers became a sign of the
love and imitation of Christ. It brought pagans and heretics from
the path of error for their own benefit. The role of Innocent III in
the Crusades is shown by his actions during the Fourth Crusade of
1204, directed at the Holy Land but ending instead in Constan-
tinople, the mission in Languedoc against the Albigensians and
the evangelization of Livonia.

The east-ward push of the Germans across the Rhine to the Elbe
and even beyond it, involved Christianization as a necessary
preliminary to colonization. The great North German archbishops
of Bremen and Magdeburg had early in the twelfth century
encouraged peaceful missions by missionaries and preachers such
as Norbert of Xanten, Vizelin of Lübeck and Otto of Bamberg in
the 1120s. In 1147, encouraged by St Bernard, a crusade was
mounted against the heathen Wends of the Baltic with either
baptism or death as the stark alternatives. Crusades along the
Baltic coast were generally hard to justify since the pagan peoples
of those regions were usually no great threat to their German
neighbours. The occasion for the Crusade against the Livonians
was, however, justified by the claim that Christianity in the newly
colonized areas around Riga and Uxhull had suffered a serious
blow. Not only were the small communities threatened by pagan
pirates but large numbers of baptisms were seen to have been
insincere. Finally, in 1198, Berthold of Loccum, second bishop of

Riga, was killed while launching the crusade.

The part played by Innocent III in the Crusade for the evangelization of Livonia was of crucial importance. From the beginning of his pontificate he showed that he was particularly attached to the idea of missions in north-eastern Europe carried out by Germans and by Danes. On 5 October 1199, Innocent authorized a crusade in defence of the nascent church in Livonia stating that, as it was endangered, it must be defended because it was the land and personal patrimony of Mary, the mother of Christ. Innocent's agents in this work of missionary endeavour, a method he used in all crusades, were Albert of Buxhövden (1199–1229), third bishop of Riga and the Cistercian missionary, Theodore of Treyden (d. 1219). The Bull of 19 April 1201, which Innocent sent to bishop Albert 'and to the brothers who were with him', established a close indentification of the regular chapter of the Church of Riga, consisting of those clerics who were still influenced in this region by the spirit of the Gregorian Reform Movement, with the mission of evangelization. The Bull proposed to reunite all the diverse missionaries of Livonia into one religious community (*unum regulare propositum*), with uniform habits and observance in order to adapt them in the most perfect way to their preaching of the Gospel. This was not only to protect the missionary clergy from any scandal but also was to have the effect of convincing the recent converts that this disparate group was, in reality, the representative of that common life lived according to the apostolic model, the *vita apostolica* and which inspired both monks and regular canons alike. The frequent citation of Acts 4: 32 that the multitude of believers had only one heart and one mind was to reinforce their unity in faith and in charity. The uniformity of their dress and their religious observances were to be the outward and visible sign. This move towards a stricter observance was to cover all aspects of the apostolic life, the *regula apostolica* and Innocent was to speak of this way of life as superior. Following the Gospel injunction of Luke 11: 3 the new missionaries were to set forth in apostolic poverty, with neither staff nor scrip, neither food nor money. This apostolic ideal was not to be allowed to lead the missionaries of Livonia to turn their backs on the life of the monk or the canon regular. They were not to become evangelical preachers. Whereas evangelical preachers of the first half of the twelfth century gave an individual message, even though accompanied by large crowds and often imitated by others, the missionaries in Livonia were to follow the pre-eminent apostolic value of the unity of communal life and for which the apostles had given the model in the Church of Jerusalem.

A Cistercian presence in Livonia was encouraged by Innocent III and in 1205, Theodore of Treyden founded the abbey of Dünamünde, at the mouth of and on the right bank of the River Duna. This, with its fortified buildings and cloister, was to be the armed heart and power-base for the future evangelization of Estonia. The problems of using the Cistercian Order, with its contemplative and retiring vocation seemed a radical change when used as a ministry to others. This was so not only in Livonia and in Estonia, but also in Sicily, Tuscany and Languedoc. Innocent, however, saw very clearly that within the austere life of a united Cistercian community, there existed that imitation of the apostles which could serve as the point of departure for an equally effective apostolic ministry.

Parallel to this development of the apostolic mission was the institution of the *Fratres Militie Christi de Livonia*, the Brothers of the Knighthood of Christ in Livonia, commonly known as the Sword Brothers and whose enterprise of military evangelism had received papal approval. The Sword Brothers emerged from a group of crusaders who, in 1202, were persuaded by Albert, bishop of Riga, to prolong their crusading vow into a religious profession taking service as a permanent garrison under his leadership. Some five years later a similar group, this time attempting to convert the Prussians who lived on the lower Vistula, came into being calling themselves the Knights of the Bishop of Prussia or the Knights of Dobryzn. These two new Orders differed from other military orders in that they were the servants of their bishops and were not autonomous. Their function, far from being the capture of the Holy Places in Palestine, was instead to be the conversion of the heathen. Their patrons were not only bishops but also popes who seemed prepared to extend the concept of the crusading vow to cover military action in defence of missions. These military monks had deliberately chosen to live in hardship. By maintaining permanent garrisons on the Rivers Duna and Vistula, they helped to secure the eventual success of missionary endeavour in those regions. It was a very long hard task, with frequent lapses back into paganism which had to be overcome by the use of force. It is important to remember that it was to the Baltic that Dominic and Diego had begged Innocent to allow them to go as missionaries.

Innocent had instead diverted them to aid the Cistercian mission in the Languedoc. Although fully understanding the importance of the Crusade to Livonia for the unity of Christendom, Innocent needed their support to aid the Cistercian mission in the Languedoc which was beginning to fail. It was equally important for the unity of the Church and much nearer its heart. Innocent could not allow the situation to deteriorate further.

The Fourth Lateran Council 1215

This greatest of the ecumenical councils of the Middle Ages was convoked on 19 April 1213, two and a half years before it opened on 1 November 1215 at the Lateran Palace in Rome. There is ample evidence that great crowds attended. An anonymous eye-witness, probably a cleric from Mainz and certainly a German, complained that he could not hear the Pope's sermon on account of the tumult and there exist several less reliable and later chroniclers who reported on the mass suffocation of bishops and abbots and certainly the aged bishop, Matthew of Amalfi, was trampled to death on the first day in the rush to enter the Church of the Lateran.

There were three plenary sessions and from them 68 reforming decrees were issued. Innocent's interventions during the proceedings were crucial and his great ability to sum up facts and arguments in judicial hearings were often admired by his contemporaries. He provided his audience with a considerable performance speaking with blunt directness and sarcasm many times during the debates whether in Latin or in the vernacular, *in volgare*. The Archbishop of Mainz was told to sit down three times and there are numerous other instances of Innocent's highly personal and unceremonious manner of speech.

In spite of these flashes of theatricality the Fourth Lateran Council produced the most important single body of disciplinary and reform legislation of the medieval Church. The traditionally accepted number of 70 constitutions coming from the Council is contradicted by short rubrics, the *rubricella*. The entry in the last part of Innocent's Register mentioned only 68 disciplinary constitutions but this may be explained by the separate promulgation of the dogmatic decrees. The drafting was done at the curia and the anonymous German eye-witness was quite correct in speaking of them as Innocent's constitutions, the *constitutiones domini papae*: they were read and adopted, not even debated in the Council. Innocent met with a strong and highly resistant body of opposition to his policies towards heretics and towards those new religious movements which he regarded as so important for the reform and regeneration of the Church. This opposition came from bishops, archbishops and the abbots of the older religious houses, all of whom felt to a certain extent threatened by the possible proliferation of new orders which they witnessed.

Canon III provided a clear statement which would allow the suppression of heresy. All heretics were condemned 'no matter by what names they are known: they may have different faces but they are all tied together by their tails since they are united by their emptiness'. In particular, all those 'having the appearance of godliness' but who had been forbidden to preach and yet still presumed to do so publicly or privately without papal authorization were to be excommunicated. Canon III referred to the reform of the pastoral ministry specifically linking it with the hearing of confession and the administration of penance. It dealt with the appointment of preachers and stressed the salutary and essential function of preaching and teaching by word and example. Suitable men, vigorous in deed and in word, were to be appointed and supported financially by bishops. It is in Canon XIII however, that we perhaps see most clearly the conservative reaction to the policies of Innocent III. Henceforward no new religious orders were to be founded in the Church and anyone who wished to enter an order was obliged to choose one of those already approved. If anyone wished to found a new religious house he was instructed to take a rule and a constitution from an approved order. This was a bitter blow to the policies of Innocent and posed a considerable problem for the mendicant orders neither of which had been approved in a formal manner prior to 1215. This expression of disquiet at the proliferation of small new orders represented an attempt to put back the clock. That this attempt failed meant that in the long run some of those who would have been assigned either to the traditional monasteries or else to heretical groups were found a place within the Church in the new orders of friars.

This Canon XIII of the Lateran Council was a challenge both to Francis and to Dominic and each reacted in a characteristically different fashion. Francis took his stand on divine revelation and the pope's oral approval before 1215. He had refused to base his order on any existing rule and thus laid his followers open to accusations of novelty and presumptious innovation. He had claimed to preach the Gospel by divine revelation and his first Rule was written largely using the language of the Gospels but with the addition of a few necessary statements for those wishing to live the religious life. In the twelve chapters of the *Regula Bullata* the balance was reversed with Biblical quotations, quotations from the Fathers, customs of the existing religious orders, passages from canon and civil law and from the Rule of St Benedict. With this Rule in 1223 Francis won formal recognition for his order. Dominic on the other hand rapidly conceived the idea of making the rule he already served, that of St Augustine, the basis for his new community and added his own regulations to it. The Order of Preachers was justified and confirmed by Honorius III in January 1217 as an order of canons regular.

The decree of Lateran IV against new orders — or against new rules as it had been interpreted — brought notorious difficulties to those religious leaders whom Innocent had formerly helped. Innocent had worked behind the scenes to allow the mendicants into the Church and Francis and Dominic were both in Rome in November 1215. A clear contrast emerged between the institutionalization of the Poor Clares for whom Innocent almost certainly made special arrangements and the absence of any such opportunity for the beguines. The *privilegium paupertatis* for the Clares made possible a new form of religious community for women not based on an existing order and was quite unique. The beguines, on the other hand, in spite of the efforts of their protectors failed to meet the 1215 deadline for papal approval. All Jacques de Vitry had been able to obtain for them was permission to live together in religious communities and to assist one another by mutual exhortation.

Canon XII of the Fourth Lateran Council brought about a great changes in the lives of Benedictine monks. Hitherto the typical non-Cluniac abbeys of the west had been entirely independent and autonomous. In theory the bishop of the diocese was charged with maintaining discipline but in practice the duty of visitation had rarely if ever been undertaken except by the occasional papal legate and in the case of exempt abbeys only a legate had the right of visitation. This complete freedom from control had led at the end of the twelfth century to a number of deplorable scandals and law-suits. To end all this the decree *in singulis regnis* instituted triennial General Chapters to be attended by the heads of all autonomous houses in each ecclesiastical province. They had the power of legislation for the whole body and the duty of appointing visitors for all houses. The chapters were to be convoked and directed by two Abbots President elected at the previous assembly. Besides unspecified general powers they had authority to direct the visitations between chapters. Their twofold duties were to reform by means of legislation and to maintain discipline by means of visitation.

The visitation system introduced in 1215 was explicitly modelled on that of the Cistercians. The Chapter appointed two or three pairs of visitors, usually themselves ruling superiors, who visited the monasteries situated in one or more dioceses. Along with this regular visitation the Lateran decree also reasserted the right and duty of the bishop to visit all exempt houses. This visitation as a means of reform was carried out on a scale which should have satisfied even the most vigorous of critics. Yet this chapter system failed in the long run to have any decisive effect on discipline. It also failed after a brief period of success to serve as a basis for additional machinery which might have given to the Benedictines leadership and a common policy. Innocent III gave to the monks and canons the best model then available, that of Cîteaux. This was soon outdated by the new model devised by Dominic. The jealous retention of autonomy and the disinclination for joint action continued in spite of this decree. The Benedictine Chapter was a large and unwieldy body recruited from houses of various sizes and diverse interests. They were provided with no clear code and no firm base as had been provided by the mother houses of Cîteaux or Prémontré and by the Master or General of the later mendicant orders. They had no effective sanctions to affect absentees or the disobedient while there was almost always a conservative body strong enough to hamstring any scheme for swift action or drastic reform. The attempts of the Augustinians to follow the decree were more successful.

The Fourth Lateran Council was a real attempt to deal with the problems for the Church arising from a questioning theology which accompanied the search for a true *vita apostolica* and which had spread widely throughout both the religious in communities and the laity in the world. The decisions it made formed the basis on which the new humanistic theology and inquisitorial methods of the middle of the thirteenth century could be applied. They were to make both Church and papacy think that they had at last successfully dealt with any danger of a separated Church which could so easily have come about on several occasions during the previous two centuries.

Conclusion

To give to the concept of reform or *reformatio* the single meaning of recovering and returning to a perfect form, which has been lost, would have been a hindrance when considering the religious events of the period covered by this book. It has been necessary to add Giles Constable's identification of a further aspect of reform, that is, the reshaping and innovation of institutions in order to stress their future and final end rather than their origins and past. Thus looking back to the gospels for the *vita apostolica* was matched by looking forward to the realization of salvation which should be the purpose of the Christian Church. At the end of this great period of search for the *vita apostolica*, with its return to the Gospels, with the spread of spirituality amongst churchmen and laity alike, with new orders and groups and with inspired individuals and at least one inspired pope, there remained in Latin Christendom only one universal Church in which this salvation was to be achieved. A period which had begun with the end of one reform movement had ended with the beginning of yet another. Through the intervening years reforms showing both aspects of the meaning given to *reformatio* were actively pursued but with no 'separated' Church at the end of it, no 'reformation' in the usually accepted sense had taken place.

What had occurred was a renewal or *renovatio* of the original purpose of the Christian faith which was to make the period of tremendous importance in the history of the Church. The first of the religious orders, the Cistercians, exemplified this. Its centralized and formalized authority had a single abbey, Cîteaux, at its head to which abbots abdicated some of their autonomy leading to a corresponding exemption from localized episcopal control. This high degree of organizational autonomy probably explains why the Cistercians became service agents of both the papacy and the institutional Church and why popes were so anxious that other groups of monks and canons should be in similar orders owing similar service to the Church and papacy. It also helps to explain why they were not eager that any further new orders should be formed which might not be so ready to accept the leadership or authority of Church and pope.

This was not the sole reason. The *renovatio* of the twelfth century had spread not only amongst monks but also amongst lay men and women, individuals as well as groups. No longer were the Church and the pope concerned solely with problems caused by lay rulers. These still existed, as was evidenced by the activities of Innocent III to increase the power of the papacy in political matters. He had no hesitation in explaining the relevant importance of sun and moon when comparing the Church with the empire and with the dominant role of the former in directing human society to its goal of peace and salvation. With the spiritual reawakening of the twelfth century many saw the search for this salvation as being their own responsibility, individually or in like-minded groups and this could often threaten danger to the Church. Such people might countenance being outside its organization. A lay *esprit de corps* could have been formed, based upon a general lay interest. This would have been both in opposition, and anti-pathetic to, the all-over clerical interest which was at that time the most effective single force in western society. A spiritual awakening among often illiterate laity, in spite of an increasing number of literate merchants in the towns, could have meant that the lay interpretations of scripture which followed were liable to error and even heresy in the dissemination of the true faith.

Innocent III, with others, saw the danger to the faith and to clerical superiority implicit in these lay movements. He also saw the danger to the Church and papacy of the proliferation of new orders. Unlike others, however, he had both the political strength and the negotiating skill to keep them all together by under-standing, by encouragement, by concession and even by an element of compulsion as required. Because of this, most of those who had been stirred by the *renovatio* did not really see their *vita apostolica* as taking place outside the Church. It is to Innocent III's credit that his actions did not face them with the alternative of having to consider so doing and this was particularly important in the case of the friars and the great benefits which they brought to the Church. Renewal or *renovatio* thus took place in western Christendom during the twelfth century without too much pain and anguish. Those who wished to impose it upon themselves through asceticism could do so and nearly all were of the opinion that personal rebirth of whatever form should take place within the existing Church and not outside it. There was to be more stress and strain in the thirteenth century when evangelical religiosity was replaced by scholastic humanism; when the Biblical Man of the *vita apostolica* was superseded by the Natural Man of the Schools.

Further reading

General

M.D. Chenu, *Nature, Man and Society in the Twelfth Century: Essays on New Theological Perspectives in the Latin West*, English translation by J. Taylor and L.K. Little (Chicago, 1968). A valuable survey of spirituality and the *vita apostolica*.

R.W. Southern, *Western Society and the Church in the Middle Ages*, in the *Pelican History of the Church* series II (London, 1970). An essential work for an understanding of the period.

L.K. Little, *Religious Poverty and the Profit Economy in Medieval Europe* (London, 1978). This up-to-date and comprehensive survey contains much valuable information with an illuminating analysis of the spiritual crisis and the development of an urban spirituality into which the mendicant orders were able to fit.

H. Grundmann, *Religiöse Bewegungen im Mittelalter* (2nd edn Darmstadt, 1970). The classic work with sections on Waldensians, Humiliati. Beguines and the Poor Clares, together with an account of Innocent III's policies. There is an Italian translation entitled *Movimenti religiosi nel Medioevo* (Bologna, 1974).

C. Morris, *The Discovery of the Individual 1050—1200* in *Church History Outlines* 5 (London, 1972). A readable and original view of the relationship of the individual and the spiritual and intellectual developments of the twelfth century.

C.N.L. Brooke, *The Monastic World 1000—1300* (London, 1974). A wide, enlightening and analytical survey with beautiful photographs.

C.W. Bynum, *Jesus as Mother: Studies in the Spirituality of the High Middle Ages*, Publications of the Center for Medieval and Renaissance Studies UCLA 16, (California, 1982). A collection of five essays on spirituality which are a fundamental contribution to this subject.

Chapter 1

B. Tierney, *The Crisis of Church and State 1050–1300* (New Jersey, 1964). Provides useful documents and a concise account of the Gregorian Reform Movement.

G. Constable, *Religious Life and Thought (11th –12th centuries)* (London, 1979) in the *Collected Studies Series* of Variorum Reprints. This contains three particularly useful articles on *Reformatio*, on the current state of Monastic Studies and on twelfth-century spirituality.

J. LeClercq, 'The Monastic Crisis of the Eleventh and Twelfth Centuries', in N. Hunt, ed., *Cluniac Monasticism in the Central Middle Ages* (London, 1971)

N.F. Cantor, 'The Crisis of Western Monasticism 1050–1130', *American Historical Review* 66 (1960–61)

E.W. McDonnell, 'The *Vita Apostolica*: Diversity or Dissent?', *Church History* 24 (1955)

G. Olsen, 'The Idea of the *Ecclesia Primitiva* in the Writings of the Twelfth-Century Canonists', *Traditio* 25 (1969)

C.W. Bynum, 'Did the Twelfth Century Discover the Individual?', *Journal of Ecclesiastical History* 31 (1980). A debate with Professor Colin Morris to which he replies in 'Individualism in Twelfth-Century Religion. Some Further Reflections', *Journal of Ecclesiastical History* 31 (1980)

C.N.L. Brooke, *Medieval Church and Society*, (London, 1971). A collection of essays with many sharp insights into the nature, aspirations and history of the Medieval Church.

Chapter 2

J. McCann, ed., *The Rule of St Benedict* (London, 1952). With the text in both English and Latin.

C.H. Lawrence, 'St Benedict and his Rule', *History* 67 (1982)

G. Constable, *Cluniac Studies* (London, 1980). Contains a whole series of essays on Cluny under Peter the Venerable as well as other more specialized studies.

H.E.J. Cowdrey, *The Cluniacs and the Gregorian Reform* (Oxford, 1970). A detailed discussion of the part played by the Cluniacs in the eleventh-century reform movement.

G. Constable and J. Kritzeck, eds., *Petrus Venerabilis 1156–1956: Studies and Texts Commemorating the Eighth Centenary of his Death* in *Studia Anselmiana* 40 (Rome, 1956).

The Benedictines in Britain, British Library Series No 3, (London, 1980). A useful book which accompanied the Fifteen Hundredth Anniversary Exhibition to commemorate the birth of St Benedict.

M.B. Pennington, ed., *The Cistercian Spirit, a Symposium*, Cistercian Studies, Series 3 (Shannon, 1970). Contains useful essays on the motives and ideals of the eleventh century monastic revival and on the spirit and aims of the founders of the Cistercian Order.

J. LeClercq, *Bernard of Clairvaux and the Cistercian Spirit*, (Kalamazoo, 1976)

D. Knowles, 'Cistercians and Cluniacs: the Controversy between St Bernard and Peter the Venerable', in *The Historian and Character and other essays* (Cambridge, 1964)

W. Williams, 'A Dialogue between a Cluniac and a Cistercian', *Monastic Studies*, Publications of the University of Manchester 262: Historical Series 76 (Manchester, 1938)

B. Golding, 'St Bernard and St Gilbert', in *The Influence of Saint Bernard*, B. Ward, ed., (Oxford, 1976). For the latest account of the Gilbertines.

J.C. Dickinson, *The Origins of the Austin Canons and their Introduction into England* (London, 1950). Remains the standard work in English on the Augustinians with a useful introduction to the canons in Europe in the first two chapters.

C.W. Bynum, 'The Spirituality of Regular Canons in the Twelfth Century: A New Approach', *Medievalia et Humanistica*, New Series IV (1973).

Chapter 3

E.S. Davison, *Forerunners of St Francis* (London, 1928). Interesting now as an antiquarian study.

R.B. Brooke, *The Coming of the Friars* (London, 1975). An excellent account of wandering preachers, Waldensians and early friars with wide-ranging documents in translation.

M.D. Lambert, *Medieval Heresy. Popular Movements from Bogomil to Hus* (London, 1977). A very useful section on Waldensians and Humiliati.

A. Gieysztor, 'La légende de saint Alexis en occident: un idéal de pauvrêté', in *Études sur l'histoire de la pauvrêté*, M. Mollat, ed., 2 vols. (Paris, 1974)

C. Thouzellier, *Catharisme et Valdéisme en Languedoc à la fin du xiie et au début du xiiie siècle* (2nd edn Louvain-Paris, 1969). A detailed account of the Waldensians with special emphasis on Durand de Huesca.

C. Morris, *Medieval Media* (University of Southampton, 1972). Discusses the impact of the song in transmitting new ideas and values.

B.M. Bolton, 'Innocent III's treatment of the Humiliati', *Studies in Church History* 8 (1971)

W.L. Wakefield and A.P. Evans, eds. and trans., *Heresies of the High Middle Ages* in the series *Records of Civilisation. Sources and Studies* LXXXI (New York, 1969). A large collection of source material including accounts of Waldensians and Humiliati.

Chapter 4

J.H. Moorman, *A History of the Franciscan Order from its origins to the Year 1517* (Oxford, 1968)

C. Esser, *Origins of the Franciscan Order* (trans. by A. Daly and T. Lynch, Chicago, 1970)

M.D. Lambert, *Franciscan Poverty: the Doctrine of the Absolute Poverty of Christ and the Apostles in the Franciscan Order 1210–1323* (London, 1961)

M.H. Vicaire, *Saint Dominic and his Times* (trans. K. Pond, London, 1964)

W.A. Hinnebusch, *A History of the Dominican Order: Origins and Growth to 1550* (New York, 1965)

G.R. Galbraith, *The Constitution of the Dominican Order 1216 to 1360* (Manchester, 1925)

C.N.L. Brooke, 'St Dominic and his first Biographer', *Transactions of the Royal Historical Society* 17 (1967)

Chapter 5

M. McLaughlin, 'Peter Abelard and the Dignity of Women: Twelfth-Century "Feminism" in Theory and Practice', in *Pierre Abelard, Pierre le Vénérable: les courants philosophiques, littéraires et artistiques en Occident au milieu de XIIe Siècle,*

Colloques internationaux du centre national de la recherche scientifique 546 (Paris, 1975)

S. Roisin, 'L'efflorescence cistercienne et le courant féminin de piété au xiiie siècle', *Révue d'histoire écclesiastique* 39 (1943).

S.P. Thompson, 'The problem of the Cistercian nuns in the twelfth and early thirteenth centuries', in *Medieval Women, Studies in Church History*, Subsidia I, ed. D. Baker (Blackwell, 1978)

R.B. Brooke and C.N.L. Brooke, 'St Clare', in *Medieval Women* as above.

E.W. McDonnell, *Beguines and Beghards in Medieval Culture with special emphasis on the Belgian scene* (New York, 1969). Much useful information but readers are recommended to use the index.

B.M. Bolton, '*Mulieres Sanctae*', *Studies in Church History* 10 (1973)

M.C. Barber, 'Women and Catharism', *Reading Medieval Studies* 3 (1977) for an enquiry into the role of women in Catharism.

Two books on Catharism for a development of this area.

J. Duvernoy, *Le catharisme: la religion des cathares* (Toulouse, 1979)

R.I. Moore, *The Origins of European Dissent* (London, 1977) who sees anti-clericalism as fundamental to the growth of heresy.

Chapter 6

G. Barraclough, *The Medieval Papacy* (London, 1968). A general account of the papacy in the twelfth century.

J.W. Baldwin, *Masters, Princes and Merchants: the social views of Peter the Chanter and his Circle* 2 vols. (Princeton, 1970) includes much detail on the Third Lateran Council.

A. Luchaire, *Innocent III. Le Concile de Latran* (Paris, 1908)

H. Tillmann, *Pope Innocent III* in *Europe in the Middle Ages*, Selected Studies vol. 12, R. Vaughan, ed., (North Holland-Amsterdam, 1980). This classic study of the pontificate of Innocent III has much useful information but the translation is hard to read.

M. Maccarrone, *Studi su Innocenzo III* in *Italia Sacra: Studi e documenti di Storia Ecclesiastica* 17 (Padua, 1972)

R. Brentano, *Rome before Avignon: a social history of thirteenth century Rome* (London, 1974)

A. Vauchez, *La Sainteté en Occident aux derniers siècles du Moyen Age: d'après les procès de canonisation et les documents hagiographiques*, École Française de Rome, Palais Farnese (Rome, 1981)

L. and J. Riley-Smith, *The Crusades: Idea and Reality 1095–1274* (London, 1981)

E. Christiansen, *The Northern Crusades: The Baltic and the Catholic Frontier 1100–1525* (London, 1980)

W. Urban, The Baltic Crusade (Illinois, 1975)

W. Urban, 'The Organization of the Defense of the Livonian Frontier in the Thirteenth Century', *Speculum* (1973)

M.H. Vicaire, 'Vie commune et apostolat missionaire. Innocent III et la mission de Livonie', in *Mélanges M.D. Chenu*, Bibliothèque Thomiste 37, (Paris 1967)

S. Kuttner and A. Garcia y Garcia, 'A new eye-witness account of the Fourth Lateran Council', *Traditio* XX (New York, 1964)

C.N.L. Brooke, 'Innocent III and Gregory IX', in *Medieval Church and Society* (London, 1971)

B.M. Bolton, 'Tradition and temerity: papal attitudes to deviants 1159–1216' in *Studies in Church History* 9 (1972)

The eye-witnesses

Libellus de Diversis Ordinibus et Professionibus qui sunt in Aecclesia, G. Constable and B. Smith, eds. and trans. (Oxford, 1972) A parallel text in Latin and in English of a work attacking and defending different types of religious life.

The Historia Occidentalis of Jacques de Vitry, J.F. Hinnebusch, ed., *Spicilegium Friburgensi* 17 (Fribourg, 1972). In Latin.

Lettres de Jacques de Vitry (1160/70 –1240), R.B.C. Huygens, ed., (Leiden, 1960) Contains the famous letter of 1216 in which he observed the Humiliati and the Franciscans on his way to Perugia. The Anonymous Chronicler of Laon, Walter Map and Burchard of Ursperg appear in an English translation in Wakefield and Evans, *Heresies of the High Middle Ages*.

S. Francis of Assisi: his Life and Writings as recorded by his Contemporaries, L. Sherley-Price (trans. London, 1959). In English.

Scripta Leonis, Rufini et Angeli Sociorum S. Francisci. The Writings of Leo, Rufino and Angelo, Companions of St Francis.

R.B. Brooke, ed. (Oxford, 1970). A parallel text in Latin and in English.

Gesta Innocentii Tertii in *Patrologia Latina* 214, J.P. Migne, ed., (Paris, 1855) for the anonymous biography and sole contemporary account of the life and deeds of Innocent III up to 1208. In Latin.

Index